HIDDEN POLITICS OF THE CRUCIFIXION

VOLUME TWO
HIDDEN TREASURE SERIES

BY
GLENN KIMBALL
DAVID STIRLAND

ANCIENT MANUSCRIPTS PUBLISHING

HIDDEN POLITICS OF THE CRUCIFIXION

COPYRIGHT © 1998

First Edition
First Printing

ISBN 1-893548-00-7
Printed in the United States of America

Cover designed by Gregg Chamberlain,
G.B. Chamberlain Sales & Advertising.

ACKNOWLEDGMENTS

I wish to thank Gregg Chamberlain for his design of the cover and his interest and encouragement in the project. I also wish to thank my father who passed in 1997 for his undying interest in history as he taught me around his knees about the history of the world. I want to thank my mother Esther for her faith and prayers and her example of unconditional love. I wish to thank my brother Tom for his consistent encouragement. I wish to thank those around the "Kitchen Table," and the frank discussion which inspired this text. I wish to thank all those who have written and called who have been lifted by the ancient texts. It has been your hunger after ancient manuscripts, which has brought this work to light. Lastly, I wish to thank all those who have participated in the creation of "ancientmanuscripts.com." Come join with us in our quest for the truth.

-- Glenn Kimball

DEDICATION

To the son of David and Beth Ann Stirland
who passed away

To the courage of David and "Sonny" whose sacrifice
and care filled his life with love

Hidden Treasure Series

Volume Two

For more information about the Hidden Treasure Series and related books and research sources contact us at "ancientmanuscripts.com."
The first volume in the series is the best seller "*Hidden Stories of the Childhood of Jesus*."

Both books can be obtained for distribution through Origin Book Sales Salt Lake City, Utah, or through the web site "ancientmanusripts.com."

The Hidden Treasure Series is designed to be a walk through history from the perspective of ancient manuscripts. It is a phenomenological view, which neither attempts to represent itself as scripture, nor as doctrine. Phenomenology looks for the smoke created by history and searches for the fire that created it. The Hidden Treasure series is written for the common reader. It is designed to take the stories from the realm of ponderous anthologies and obscure hidden texts and out of the hands of the faithless scholars and protective believers and lay it at the feet of the people. The reader will have an instant sensation that the rest of the phenomena of faith finally make sense. The hidden agenda of "The Series" is to return the world back to their own traditions better prepared to understand. Between the lines is a reason for faith. In a small way it is the fulfillment of the prophecy of Jesus, which said that in the end, "That which was hidden will ultimately be made manifest." I can not guarantee that everything in the manuscripts is true, only that the manuscripts exist and that the stories shaped the unspoken course of Christianity for two thousand years. We can deny that the manuscripts are real if we choose, but we can't deny that they have had an impact on the Christian world behind the scenes.

Pontius Pilate and his wife Claudia Procula have been maligned in history and film, though they have been vindicated in our ancient and modern religious practices. Their story deserves to be told.

The story of the arrest of Joseph of Arimathea and his involvement in the crucifixion is long overdue. He is the unsung hero of all times. Nicodemus played a role in the life of Jesus as best friend of the great Joseph of Arimathea. His records, which preserved these tales, have been badly abused and ignored. Perhaps through his loyalty he will someday be restored to his rightful place in history along with the most famous family who ever lived.

Contents

Where Were the Apostles during the Crucifixion?

Section 9. Conclusion

The Healing of Tiberius Caesar
This Old Man's Thought

Bibliography

OBJECTIVES OF THIS BOOK

TWO MAJOR OBJECTIVES

There are two objectives to this book, as is the case in each of the books in this series. The first is to tell the "hidden" stories surrounding the death of Jesus, including the fate of His persecutors and reveal the true identity of the guilty that were actually responsible for His death. The whole story of Easter involves much more than the limited history contained within the Bible. The best parts of Easter over 2,000 years have even been left out of our oral traditions. This history comes to us from forgotten ancient manuscripts. The Jews, as a culture and religion, were not responsible for Jesus' death. In fact, the majority of Jews at the time of Jesus were his advocates.

The second objective of this book is designed to encourage the reader, once again, to enter this vast and legitimate world of extra-Biblical Christian documents. These old documents found outside the Bible are not "evil" as has been suggested by naïve clergy. For too long there has been a conspicuous double standard for historical writings related to the life of Jesus. Why is it so easy for some to accept the Bible completely and yet reject the surrounding documents with vehemence? It doesn't make sense logically or spiritually. It hasn't made sense for 2,000 years.

None of us would myopically question the histories of Julius Caesar who pre-dated Jesus by a generation. The same type of history chronicles both Julius and Jesus. However, we have thrown the histories of Jesus summarily out the window because the clergy of the third century voted to exclude them from the canon. In most cases extra-Biblical histories are more revealing than Biblical accounts. It was never the intent of those who penned the books of the Bible to suggest that their writings were the only histories in existence. To ignore parts of Christian history merely because councils of Nicea didn't sanctioned them is childish. Yet that is exactly what we have done. Ignoring the rest of these histories will speak louder to our generation of our prejudices and narrow mindedness than ever before. We are the generation with the option to view declassified documents and evaluate them for ourselves. Deep inside we should have expected for centuries that a day would come when we would have MORE.

Modern Christians have forgotten the reasons for the original councils of Nicea who gave us the Bible. Those councils were held to arbitrate a great historical argument and to gather Christian power together under specific leadership. At the time there were greater numbers of fragmented Christian sects than there are today. Each had their unique beliefs and diverse sacred writings. Literally thousands of documents were excluded from the Bible. The great Arius was under condemnation at that time for telling the Christian world that there were greater numbers of precious writings than were being considered by the clergy of the day. Historians like Eusebius, the Father of ecclesiastical history, who were allies of Arius, weren't even invited to the councils to give their evidence of the existence of "more." When Constantine literally sat in judgment between the two great factions of Christianity (those who liked the "more" and those who liked the "less"), he locked the door to Christian history with the word "heresy." Someone should have defined for him what real heresy meant. Those who stole the rest of the histories from us perpetrated the real heresy. Who was Constantine that he thought he could arbitrate that fight as if he were some ecclesiastical head of The Church? How could we allow him to limit our understanding of that history? Arius wasn't writing secret lies in his basement by himself. The histories he advocated were widely accepted documents written by the original apostles and family of Jesus. Among other things, they spoke of the heresy "entering the flock" after the crucifixion. No wonder these documents were banned. Constantine didn't like to consider himself a member of the wolf pack. When the gavel of Constantine came down at the conclusion of the councils of Nicea, history was permanently altered. The whole truth was buried and limited for millennia and those with real heresy in their hearts had won. We still see fingerprints of the heresy in prophecies of Jesus remaining in the Bible. The wolves did enter the flock sparing no one that opposed them. (Acts 20:29) We are the ones who continue to allow the wolves their ill-gotten gain when we refuse to read the rest.

Yet we shouldn't confuse the wolves among the flock with modern religious institutions. What happened in history was the fault of an ancient people and not of sincere men who are pursuing their God today. To begin with, Arius' contention was not that the institutions were evil. He merely felt that some of their behaviors "short sheeted" the real history of Jesus. Arius finally gave up in order to maintain his connection with the faith. If we are looking for perfection, Jesus himself couldn't find that among His chosen twelve. We shouldn't be so willing to make the mistake of Constantine by throwing babies out with the bath water. It's easy to see the historical "beam" in the eyes of the Council of Nicea and miss the modern "mote" in our own. That mote has caused us to squint when it comes to Christian history.

For a long time we should have expected that modern research would substantially add to what we have been "spoon fed" through our traditions. The real miracle of modern discoveries is that they not only validate the divinity of Jesus, but also answer many of our most private religious questions.

What are we afraid of? That is the most important question that both believers and non-believers must ask themselves. Are the unbelievers afraid they will find a miracle? Are the believers afraid that someone didn't tell them about all the miracles? Are we afraid that Jesus will be reduced to the status of "myth?" Sadly, by ignoring history, both sides have already done that. The expanding story is evidence of the need for a renewed faith beyond that which was offered to us by our ancestors. It is too late to be afraid that more will be found. The gaps in the story are beginning to close and both sides of this ancient controversy will eventually be embarrassed if they turn their heads. The miracle of our time is that no one person or institution is powerful enough to keep hidden these "secrets" any longer. The common man will have his day - and that day is today.

4

WHY HAVEN'T WE HEARD THESE THINGS BEFORE?

There are those who will ask, "Why haven't we heard of these startling facts before, given the tens of thousands of Christian writers over 2,000 years?" As this story has unfolded, this has been a shock to us as well.

The answer to that question comes in three parts. First, the histories contained in this book have long existed in remote corners of libraries, but have been ignored. People didn't like to brag about the "heresies" they had hidden in their libraries.

By no means are we the first to say what we are about to say. Some naïve critics have suggested that this material is of questionable origin, but it now appears that the reasons for hiding this material are far more dubious than the history itself. We all agree that the writing of history is an imperfect science under the most favorable conditions. We have expected our histories of Jesus to be perfect far too long and have found them to be imperfect in the end. The expanding discoveries of Jesus can no longer be dismissed based on an argument of perfection, because they have a momentum of their own, with multiple cross-referenced sources that contain an important flavor that has been wrongfully overlooked.

To ignore principle facts of history because they conflict with tradition is inexcusable. After all, tradition itself has been as fluid as the writing of history and has changed over time with a variety of external pressures. When cross-referenced from a variety of independent sources, this history enjoys a divergent base of scholarly support. When an historian begins to encounter the same tales told by a variety of people, the fulcrum, or main ingredients, becomes credible. This history is not the account of one specific perspective, but rather the composite of many. Similar stories are told by diverse groups of people with their own agendas and traditions.

There is an old logic used by critiques that says when you put 20 people in a line and whisper the story in the ear of the first, when the story is told by the last person, it has significantly changed. That is exactly what has happened to the scriptures. However, let's add a new wrinkle to that logic. Let's take 20 lines, with 20 people in each, and tell the same story. By the time it reaches the end of each line, the stories will differ. However, if you take the common points from each of the resulting stories, you can reconstruct the original tale with some accuracy. That is exactly why this history is so critical. We need more histories, not fewer, in order to find the truth.

The real problem with the following narrative is that there isn't an adequate foundation for these accounts within tradition. Through the centuries many of these stories didn't make sense to historians who didn't know the whole truth, so they were discarded. Some of the details have been like leaves found on the ground with no tree in sight. We need to find the tree in order to understand these leaf-like stories. Hopefully this history will provide a framework on which to graft these isolated fragments surrounding the history from the crucifixion of Jesus. The reader will have the sensation that finally some of the answers to his or her own private questions begin to emerge from obscurity and make sense. The history of Jesus is so full of paradox that the common public hasn't even known what questions to ask.

6

Secondly, even the believers have been looking in all the wrong places for a history of Jesus that extends far beyond Palestine. The history of Jesus should never have been assumed to come exclusively from "The Holy Land." Some of the players were from different parts of the world. It is important to understand that a history isolated to Palestine was easier to control by the "protectors of the word" than one extending throughout the known world. None of the emerging faiths wanted to merge their relationship with Jesus with other traditions. They told the stories that belonged to them and ignored the rest.

Lastly, there has been a traditional conflict between the two major camps of historians that wrote about Jesus. The truth is in the middle ground that both sides have declared "No man's land." One camp includes the priestly scribe-like historians; the other group includes the atheistic scholars. The faithless scholars have found the history but have refused to recognize the miracle that it contains. What use is a miraculous history to those who are irrevocably predisposed to think that Jesus was a myth? The Christians haven't included this history contained within their own discarded writings because they have feared that it might conflict with personal religious traditions. Most of the rest of us are simply bystanders in this conflict willing to listen to both sides as long as we are allowed to make up our own minds. However, the freedom to make up our own minds has been stolen from us with the hiding of these written histories.

Sadly, it appears that men on both sides are often more protective of their traditions about Jesus than they are of truth. It has been difficult for both sides to "let go" and let the story lead us where it may. Happily, in the end, it leads us back to a faith in Jesus, whether or not it resembles the history we have been taught from religious or educational podiums. Both podiums stand high above their respective congregations and treat the common man, and his rational abilities and his relationship with his maker, with impunity.

CONTENTS OF THIS HISTORY

The first of the extra-Biblical texts included in this work are the letters between Pontius Pilate and Herod and the letters of Pilate to both Tiberius and one of the "Augustus" Caesars.

The word "Augustus" was a title more than a name. There were several Caesars that used the title, and some of them lived contemporarily with other Caesars who were the acting heads of state. They often used the title "Augustus" like a retired Caesar emeritus. The real name of the Augustus at the time of the birth of Jesus was Octavian - the same Octavian who earlier in his life had shared the rule of Rome with Mark Anthony. Mark Anthony was the one who met his demise at the hands of Octavian because of his divisive passion for Cleopatra. It is strange to note that Augustus/Octavian was publicly a family man, though he had his discrete illicit affairs. His personal residence was atypical for a Roman Emperor. Most of the others basked in spectacular luxury and debauchery, but not Augustus/Octavian. The movie "Cleopatra" badly misrepresented the characters of both Mark Anthony and Augustus/Octavian. Mark Anthony was the wild monarch with a passion for opulence and lust, and Octavian Caesar lived a relatively modest home life for a man with such power and wealth.

These letters reveal the startling fact that Tiberius, the adopted son of Augustus/Octavian and one of the subsequent Augustus Caesars, eventually came to know Jesus far better than we have previously understood. When they both came to know The Christ, it changed each of their lives forever.

The second part of the extra-Biblical writings includes excerpts from the canonical Nicodemus. This seemingly obscure Pharisee mentioned in the Bible physically attended the real trial of Jesus. There are rumors that Nicodemus was a relative of the family, which makes sense given the evidence and the clannish nature of the time. Nicodemus was an extremely powerful and fabulously wealthy Jewish Sanhedrin councilman. We should have long expected that some of the large and powerful family of Jesus would have been seated on the most prestigious religious councils of the time, even the one that supposedly condemned Him to the cross. We have not commonly expected Jesus' family to also be seated on the powerful councils of Rome itself.

Joseph of Arimathea, the best friend of Nicodemus and the great uncle of Jesus, was a provincial Roman Senator. This story tells us what happened to him during the crucifixion that kept him from saving the life of his grand nephew.

Joseph of Arimathea and Nicodemus were a much larger part of the story of the crucifixion than Biblical history records. They almost changed the entire face of contemporary religion with their influence. Had Joseph of Arimathea and Nicodemus been successful, an ancient "chosen family" would not have separated in two. (Christian/Jew) These two men had gone to the floor of the Sanhedrin three years before the death of Jesus to seek the support of their fellow councilmen to adopt the writings and sayings of Jesus into Jewish tradition. The surprise of our times is to learn that they had the votes behind them on the Jewish Sanhedrin Council to begin the great religious transition into a living faith that they had envisioned! Joseph of Arimathea also had the financial and political power to influence Rome. After all, he was given the title of Noblis Decurio by Caesar himself and sat as a provincial Roman Senator. However, something very dark and sinister occurred that plunged Christians and Jews into isolation from each other for almost two 2,000 years and caused Pilate to act independently from those with Roman position who wanted to spare Jesus' life.

Sadly, history has seen religion feed on itself to the point that it could no longer integrate "real time" religious events into their well-established traditions. For example, the Jews had adjusted to, and controlled, their dead prophets by the time of Jesus. However, they struggled with their "prophet" while He was living among them, as He healed their sick and raised their dead. There were many at the time of Jesus, especially the Sadducees, who were just waiting for an excuse to exclude Jesus from their traditions and oppose Joseph of Arimathea and Nicodemus. The momentum of the day was to include Jesus, but any full integration of His life and teachings meant serious financial consequences for the reigning Sadducees who were being paid by the Romans to lead the Jews. Jesus continued to be accepted by the Jews as a prophet, and pieces of His story now fit comfortably along side the rest of the fragments of the stories of their other DEAD prophets. The whole story now rings like the blast from an ancient trumpet that brings lifeless tradition to rubble, revealing the need for a living oracle in their midst.

We should not single out the Jews in this behavior, because Christians, Moslems, Hindus and other world religions that believe in parts of the saga of Jesus have followed in the footsteps of the Jews. It has been easy to see the "mote" in the eye of the Jew while missing the "beam" in our own.

We find ourselves once again in an age of spectacular fulfillment of prophecy spoken from the mouths of the holy prophets, and Jesus himself, for thousands of years. It is the modern faithful Christians who now must listen and make a place in our minds for a faith that will shortly spring to life once again. Will we understand the events of our world when the heavens present the final scenes of this earth as we know it? Will we do any better in "real time" than the Jews did when Jesus walked among them? Will we have forgotten the whole story of the crucifixion by the time He returns and refuse to listen as it is being rediscovered?

This book is not intended to cover every detail of the crucifixion of Jesus. There are tens of thousands of volumes written by scholars and churchmen around the worlds in all eras of time, which make a complete story impossible between the covers of any single work. Mostly this book is designed to illustrate the depth of extra-Biblical research that is available to modern believers. The discoveries in this book are designed to awaken the sleeping hearts of the masses and cast their eyes to the horizons of their personal vigil for the coming of the living Messiah in our time.

We all know something about the excruciating demise of Jesus from the Bible. "Now for the rest of the story!"

IMPORTANT QUESTIONS TO ASK AS YOU READ THIS BOOK

When you really think about it, there have been inconsistencies in the traditional versions of the life and death of Jesus which haven't made sense for 2,000 years. For example:

- Where are the Biblical records of the life of Jesus between the age of 12 and the beginning of His adult ministry?
- Where are the Roman accounts of the crucifixion?
- Why did Jesus appear like a stranger among a people who obviously knew about the miraculous and well-known events surrounding His birth?
- How could Jesus' own people, who knew and loved Him, allow Him to be crucified in their own midst?
- Why would the Bible tell us at least two different and contrasting versions of the crucifixion of Jesus? Which one is the truth, and does it make a difference to us today?
- Why did the murderous Romans, who slaughtered the Christians and Jews in public spectacles following the death of Jesus, ultimately become the defenders of the faith?

- Why would the Romans return to Judea and massacre an already conquered people right after Jesus' death? Why would the Romans want to exterminate the operators of the most modern seaport in the world made of underwater concrete (the first of its kind)? Was NERO's fire the real reason Rome threw the Christians and Jews to the lions?
- Why did the Jews pick this particular time in history to rise up with their little armies to face the most formidable army the world had ever known?
- Why did Christians later venerate Pontius Pilate and his wife Claudia Procula? Pilate and his wife are still considered as Saints in the Byzantine Christian tradition and are officially considered "innocent and virtuous figures" by the Catholic tradition.
- Why did Pilate come to the defense of a Messiah figure that he was sent to find and eliminate in the first place? Did Pilate know Jesus long before he allowed Him to be crucified?
- How did Pilate die? Is it possible that he died in the defense of Jesus?
- Did Tiberius Caesar know about Jesus and want him to die?
- Who was really responsible for the death of Jesus? Why did they want Him dead?
- What was this guard that was used to arrest Jesus if Pilate wanted to wash his hands of the whole thing after the arrest was made?

- Why were there so many Christians following Jesus' death, when our common Biblical perceptions of these events leave us with the impression that there were few defenders of Jesus during His lifetime?
- Why did the very people who threw palms before Jesus on his entrance to Jerusalem chant for His death a few hours later?
- Where were the defenders of Jesus when He was crucified?
- Why did the Romans let the Jewish Sanhedrin retain a strong police force and leave the Herod Dynasty intact during the era of Jewish rebellion?
- Why couldn't the powerful and wealthy family of Jesus save Him from the crucifixion? Where was the powerful and influential Joseph of Arimathea, the great uncle of Jesus, when he was being crucified?

The list goes on and on. Our common Biblical story of the events is obviously inadequate! The letters and extra-Biblical texts included in this document provide some of the critical missing pieces of the puzzle that transform these enigmas into meaningful realities.

THE EARLY YEARS OF JESUS

INTRODUCTION

There are non-practicing Christians walking every street today who have secretly asked the question of themselves, "Was Jesus who He said He was?" Somewhere deep inside many of us have felt, at one time or another, that if we knew for sure that Jesus was the Christ, it would change the way we do everything in our lives. Admittedly, it has been very difficult for the general public to digest and assimilate a story that contains numerous and needless discrepancies that have been cloaked in the garb of controversy and "heresy." There are many naïve atheists who actually question whether or not Jesus even existed. The history of Jesus is no less prominent in the libraries of ancient texts than that of the Caesars.

The eventual merger of Rome and the church is evidence that both histories are inalterably mingled together. The Caesars have wrongfully born the blame for His crucifixion for millennia. The Caesars eventually considered the history of Jesus as their own personal history, and there is strong reason to believe that they were right. The headquarters of Christianity were moved from Jerusalem to Rome because they considered the history as a Roman history. This was no coincidence. The only question left for the common public is why did the Romans consider the life and times of Jesus their own history? The answer is clear. The Romans had more history of Jesus than was contained in the early writings of Josephus, the Jewish traitor who sat at the tables of the early Caesars in Rome and wrote paid historical apologies for the Romans.

There were many contemporaries of Jesus who asked the same personal question, "Was Jesus really the Messiah." Many of them had the spectacular opportunity to find the answer to that one question for themselves. Surprisingly, the Governor Pilate, who bore a portion of the responsibility for allowing Jesus to be crucified, was one of those people. Common Christian history ignores the fact that Pilate met the resurrected Jesus face-to-face just outside of Jerusalem. That history and dialogue are included below. When Pilate saw the crucifixion marks on a living Jesus, it brought him to his knees, changed his world, and later cost him his life.

Some modern Christian historians have faithlessly suggested that Jesus was taken from the cross -- alive. There is so much evidence that Jesus wandered the streets of Palestine after His death that it has often appeared to the faithless scholars that someone was merely playing a crucifixion trick on us. The post-crucifixion history of Jesus' ministry is strewn from one side of the earth to the other. The resurrected Christ appeared before isolated pockets of the faithful until the middle sixth century. When he finally ended that part of His ministry, He spoke of the spiritual darkness that would cover the earth. Indeed that is one of the reasons we call this period of time the "Dark Ages."

Pilate knew that Jesus had been killed on the cross, so he was shaken when he saw Jesus alive again walking the earth. We have to ask ourselves why would Christians leave such an event out of the Bible? They obviously believed in these events or they wouldn't have risen Pilate to the status of Sainthood. The real answer is that they only half ignored it. The Byzantine and Coptic Christians have canonized Pilate. The Catholics have made Pilate an "innocent and virtuous figure" in history because of Pilate's meeting with the resurrected Jesus. There are many fine Catholics today who pray openly to Pilate as an advocate to God. How much more Christian history has been ignored and left out of the Bible?

It was frightening for Tiberius to see the dead of Rome walking the streets when Jesus was resurrected. Jesus wasn't the only one of the dead to rise at that time. However, Christian historians omit those accounts from the Bible as well. However, they couldn't eliminate them from the Roman histories. There were several accounts of destruction and terror in Rome during those three days of darkness while Jesus lay in the tomb of His great uncle, Joseph of Arimathea. Tiberius looked for someone to blame after the heavens shook and the dead walked the streets of Rome. Many of the ancient Roman tombs were permanently sealed at that time to keep the dead from rising. We are just beginning to find those empty tombs beneath Rome today.

Tiberius turned to his grandson, through marriage, for some answers to the catastrophes in Rome. When Tiberius found out that his grandson Pilate had played a role in allowing Jesus to be crucified, it cost Pilate his life. This is especially true when we find out that Tiberius had sent for Jesus to come to Rome to heal him of his personal affliction. That letter didn't arrive in time to save the life of Jesus. Tiberius wanted to vindicate the death of the man who had raised the dead from the tombs in Rome and frightened his people. Therefore, he sent his legions to begin the extermination of infant Christianity. Christians were

17

being martyred long before Nero burn Rome to the ground and blamed the Christians. We have long wrongfully blamed the burning of Rome for the martyrdom of Christianity in the early years.

Those that suggest Jesus was taken down from the cross before His demise never tell you where He is buried today, nor why there continued to be sightings of the resurrected Jesus until the middle of the sixth century. He either was the oldest living man since before the flood of Noah, or the resurrected Savior was whom He claimed to be. It will do little good to call these accounts myth when we see that the world has preserved divergent accounts of His post-crucifixion ministry.

What a surprise it must have been for Pilate to meet and speak to the man whom he had indirectly killed. When Pilate met the resurrected Jesus, it was clear from their conversation that Jesus had been crucified and that Pilate was most repentant. There are startling writings of friends and foes alike that tell the same tale.

We all know from the Bible about some of Jesus' sensational healings and His incomprehensible raising of the dead, but few understand that the vast majority of the healings and the raisings from the dead happened after Jesus was crucified. Our Biblical accounts end before the best of the story begins.

The events of Jesus' post-mortal life were confounded in history by the fact that the remaining disciples of Jesus were expelled from Palestine right after His death by the ruling Sadducees in the Exodus of the Faithful in 36 AD. The Romans finished that disbursement of the disciples to the four winds with their attempts at total genocide of the persecutors of Jesus. Much of the post-crucifixion story emerges in some unexpected places because it couldn't possibly have been written in their home country, which was under siege at the time. No wonder we have to look far beyond Palestine for the truth.

Joseph of Arimathea, Jesus' great uncle, would never have fled Palestine after the crucifixion with the Mother Mary without Jesus if He had still been alive. Joseph left the country in 36 AD with Mary, Lazarus, Mary Magdalene, The Bethany Sisters, Martha and others. Surely, he would have taken Jesus with him if for no other reason than for Jesus' protection. After all, Joseph of Arimathea had acted as Jesus' father since the death of Joseph, Mary's husband, when Jesus was about 15 years old. The candid reality is that Jesus had been both crucified and then resurrected. This is the only explanation that fits the mountains of recorded evidence.

The world of the apostles didn't change until after they saw those marks on the hands, feet, and side of the resurrected Lord. The resurrection of Jesus is what really launched Christianity. However, most of the stories of Jesus from the Bible end at the crucifixion. Some of the apostles needed to see those marks before they were willing to continue their ministry. Most of them had run home when Jesus was crucified and were nowhere to be found when the "deed" was done. John, the best friend of Jesus, was the only one that continued through the night of the crucifixion with his Friend. Even Peter slipped away after he denied knowing Him three times.

There have been others all around the world that also saw the marks on the resurrected Lord. The legend of His post-crucifixion visits in many foreign lands, have been recorded in the writings of a "Martyred Savior" in locations far distant from Palestine. Prophecy has foretold that all the children of God will eventually see those same marks, and someday "Every knee shall bow and every tongue confess that Jesus is the Christ." There is a lot of story telling left to do. Those who have sealed and limited their interest within the Bible pages will miss the best of the story yet to come. We need to consider our day to be similar to the day of Jesus in that we are expecting His Second Coming as they were expecting His first. For this reason alone, many of the same problems exist in our day as existed in the day of the mortal life of Jesus. We have ignored our history of the Messiah as the Jews ignored theirs.

Something wonderful happened five centuries after the death of Jesus, at the time of the fall of the Roman Empire. Much of the truth about the hidden histories of Jesus was declassified and returned to the scholars from the hidden vaults of the Vatican by the Goths and Visgoths. The Goths and Visgoths had a personal reason for preserving the ancient manuscripts about the life and times of Jesus because they too had the royal blood of the House of David in their veins. Jesus was family to them. It is clear from those records the extent of the ancient manuscripts were in the possession of Constantine in the third century. By this time the Bible had already flooded the world, and there was no one to restore sacred records back into the Bible where they had belonged in the first place.

The fifth century was also the general time of the dictation of the Koran by Gabriel to Mohammed. Strangely, much of the Koran is word-for-word the same account written by the brothers of Jesus centuries before. It was also the time, according to legend, of the appearance of King Arthur. Most scholars today agree that there were

20

probably several real King Arthur's. Strangely, King Arthur, a descendant of the family of Jesus, also predicted that he, too, would someday return to this world, as he believed his ancestor the Messiah would. That caption was written on the lid of his lead-lined tomb, the lead mined from the estate of the family of Jesus. The real tomb of this great King Arthur was moved to protect it from vandals and is the reason King Arthur has long been considered a myth. There have been many that have looked for the "Holy Grail" and would have dug up King Arthur to find it.

When the tales of Jesus' appearances ceased after the sixth century, a real darkness covered the earth, but the story of the "Dark Ages" will be the subject of another book in this series.

THE EASTER STORY BEGINS

The true story of Spanish-born Pontius Pilate from Seville is so sensational that no fictionalized novel could compare. It has bizarre elements of horror that Steven King would envy. It speaks of incest that makes soap operas seem virtuous. It has adventure that makes the fictional Indiana Jones seem like a Boy Scout at summer camp. Most paradoxically, it is a story of an acknowledgment of the divinity of Jesus from a perspective that is unprecedented in the annals of Christendom.

The Easter story actually begins when Pilate was made the Governor of Palestine, like a wedding present from his wife's grandfather, Tiberius Caesar. Pilate was sent to the newly conquered territory of the Roman Eastern Province to investigate, and control, the rumors of a possible covert rebellion among the Jews. This rumored uprising centered on the growing belief of a prophesied king that had been born in the midst of the Jews during the reign of Herod the King in Palestine and Augustus/Octavian Caesar in Rome.

This King of Israel had been on the lips of the prophets for thousands of years. It had been on the lips of every culture known to man. Tiberius Caesar was a very superstitious man who placed credence in such tales. We can be sure that whether or not Tiberius believed the rumors himself, he was convinced that Herod and the Jews believed them, and so did the majority of the known world. Tiberius may not have believed in the coming of a Messiah King, but his granddaughter Claudia Procula, the wife of Pilate, convinced him that Jesus could heal the sick.

It is extremely likely that one of the reasons that Pilate was chosen to govern the Roman Eastern Province was because Pilate was well versed in the legends of the Messiah King. He had studied in the great open air Druid University in England where they, too, had been expecting their Messiah King to come into the world. Their Messiah had a name -- "Hesus," unlike the Messiahs from other traditions. The Druids had built a temple in Jerusalem more than 2,000 years BC in just such anticipation. Pilate was well drilled in the legends of the Messiah because of his college training and was the perfect choice for the Eastern Province post.

In his studies Pilate had encountered the tales of Jesus who had spent a great deal of time in the ancestral home of Jesus' grandmother Saint Anna -- England, where the Druid University with 60,000 students was located. The Druid universities rivaled the great seat of learning in

22

Alexandria, Egypt, and probably had more students. The Romans depended greatly on the Druid Universities for many of their noble scholars and for the training of Royalty in some cases. There are manuscripts that record Jesus and Pilate speaking to each other in the Druid tongue at the time of the crucifixion and exchanging secret Druid passwords that were required to enter the high-level debates at the University. They both had obviously attended such conferences. These documents have long been an enigma -- even heresy -- because scholars have wondered why Jesus and Pilate would have a conversation with each other in the Druid language. These passwords were used as secret signs of brotherhood much like the secret tokens of fraternal orders today. Pilate was obviously trying to help Jesus at the time of the crucifixion, but Jesus resisted his help and was resigned to His destiny.

There is emerging evidence that not only did Pilate clearly understand and know the family of Jesus that were still in ancient England when Pilate was going to school, but that he had met Jesus personally at the university where Jesus was a prominent guest after the death of Joseph. Jesus often visited the homeland of His grandmother and had prophetically built a famous retirement home for His own mother out of Wattle Wood. The relatives of Jesus were the "rich boys" in town. They employed many people in their mining operations. How could Pilate not have known the family, and probably Jesus himself, long before the crucifixion?

The Druids have fallen into the category of many religious traditions, which we judge based on their condition at the time of their demise, rather than perceiving them from their point of origin. We have thrown many babies out

23

with the bath water in our hindsight critique. The Druids evolved into nature worshipers and have often been linked with the inception of witchcraft. But the original Druids were anything but witches. They were expecting their Messiah too.

Many modern Christians have condemned the Gnostics for exactly the same reason. The Gnostics evolved into a sexual cult with bizarre ceremonies and dark intrigue. However, the origins of the Gnostic movement were definitely Christian and were even attended by Jesus and His Apostles in person. After all, the Essenses lived in Edom just outside Jerusalem -- a short walk in those days. The Gnostics emerged from, and were mingled with, the "Essene Movement" of *Dead Sea Scroll* fame. The clothing worn by Jesus reflected his personal ties to the communal societies of the Essenes. The Great Gnostic Teacher of Righteousness is very likely Jesus Himself. We have very good translations of the writings of the great "Teacher of Righteousness." Those who think that Jesus never wrote a book obviously think either that He couldn't write, which was untrue, or that He just didn't write, which is a lie as well. Why aren't the writings of Jesus in the New Testament? Why didn't someone search for them at the time of the Nicene Council? It doesn't help to blame Constantine. We should blame ourselves for not looking for His writings, or tolerating them when we did find them.

Tiberius was also convinced that not only did the Druids and the Jews believe in the prophesied Messiah, but also others, like the Magi, had numerous tales of the generic Messiah legends. Some of these lands were under the "proctorship" of the Roman Empire, and some where still on the "acquisition list." No wonder they were well

24

informed about the perceived threat of the Messiah King. We will find in our day that the East had more plentiful records about the Coming of the Messiah than we tolerate within Christianity.

As expected, Herod Antipas, the son of Herod the King, reported to Tiberius many trends and disturbances within Judea. However, Herod was not Tiberius' only source for information. The superstitious Tiberius had a residence filled with the most serious historians and astrologers of his day. By the time of the crucifixion, Tiberius was very familiar with the birth of the Messiah. These tales spoke of the ultimate political independence of the descendants of the House of Israel led by the coming of a Messiah. The prophetical "Second Coming" of the Messiah was hard to understand since many of them hadn't understood the "First Coming" to begin with. The astrologer community spoke to each other from many places around the world and was linked with the Magi Kings that visited shortly after the birth of Jesus. The entire world rumbled at that time with the news of the Messiah. The very composition of the Magi Kings themselves was evidence of the intercultural clannish nature of the historian-astrologer world at that time.

We view astrology today as a fringe science because of the pseudo mystical practices of our day. However, the study of the stars originally included the study of geography, history and religion. The prophets used the stars to mark significant events like we would use the calendar. They also used the stars to speak of enigmatic destinations, like captains of ships on a sea. They used the stars to pinpoint prophecy because they didn't have universal calendars that could earmark dates for use between cultures. Astrology was highly developed by the time of Jesus and was the pragmatic science of the day. We are constantly finding that the very architecture of the kings was based on the stars and had been so for millennium prior to that time. The alignment of their holy places with the movements of the stars lets us know how serious they were. The fact that the birth of Jesus was earmarked by the appearance of the Star of Bethlehem is but a small piece of evidence that this Messiah was an intercultural phenomenon, and intended to be so by the prophet originators of the tales.

THE MAGI, KEY TO UNDERSTANDING JESUS

Herod the King had searched intensely for the prophesied child, after the nomadic Magi from the East had come to herald the event that so many had anticipated for thousands of years. However, he died in four BC before he could locate the Baby King. Jesus was obviously born before four BC. The infighting for political power among the sons of Herod the King after his death had effectively ended the search for the baby Jesus. This allowed Jesus to spend His childhood in relative peace amongst His own people.

After the death of Joseph Jesus spent the majority of his young adult life outside Palestine on the boats of His great uncle Joseph of Arimathea. If we want to learn about that era of His life, we need to look somewhere else besides the Bible. The Holy Family returned from Egypt where Jesus was a local sensation among the fragmented houses of Pharaoh. However, as Jesus grew to a young man, His exploits were much more difficult to camouflage from the

Herod Dynasty. It wasn't coincidence that Jesus had the opportunity to sail the world with His great uncle, Joseph of Arimathea.

After the death of Joseph, when Jesus was about 15, Jesus sailed the world, which kept His life and deeds discrete and protected until His permanent return to Palestine to begin His final ministry. The early manhood of Jesus was something hard to trace because of all his travels. Jesus' travels also kept His early years from our traditions held sacred in the canon. We are just beginning to understand the last verse in the Gospel of John -- Jesus' best friend. Look it up for yourselves and let the hair stand up on the back of your neck as it did mine the first time I read it in the Bible. The exploits of Jesus during His lifetime could fill the world with history and, in fact, does.

His extra-Judean ministry is the subject of an emerging and amazing body of research. Jesus appears here and there in diverse locations conducting business for his family, healing the sick, raising the dead, walking on many waters and beginning a ministry filled with teachings of love and peace. There are no similar legends from any other specific period in history. We should have recognized the similarity of these legends and connected them back to Jesus long ago. His teachings also included a panorama of insights into agriculture, architecture, and many other sciences. Jesus was a most learned man, so we shouldn't be confused by the fact that He didn't limit His teachings to religion when He visited and taught the people of the world. The white sails of the family owned boats with the oars sticking out the sides appeared in dozens of places around the world. In each of these locations His visits were so spectacular that the legends persist today in the Holy Books of more than a dozen cultures. The Jesus phenomena is greater that the "local myth" spoken of by modern faithless skeptics.

Augustus/Octavian was undoubtedly worried when the familiar eastern monarchs confirmed the rumors that the prophesied "King of Israel" had finally been born. They had looked for Him from time-to-time, but Jesus was nowhere to be found. It is extremely likely that Tiberius had heard of Jesus' exploits from many places where Jesus traveled. I'm sure Tiberius wasn't as concerned with Jesus' behavior in foreign lands not under the Roman banner until Jesus returned to Palestine for His last three years. Perhaps Tiberius even hoped that Jesus would remain abroad. The Romans began their vigil in serious only when Jesus was walking again about the Eastern Province healing the sick and performing miracles that caused a sensation to be reckoned with by Caesar. As you will see later, Tiberius changed his tune when he fell ill himself and needed a personal healer.

The Magi played an important function in history. Groups like these had diffused prophecy from one country to another, and had settled local disputes, almost like wandering bands of powerful troubadours. They were like political and religious ambassadors among the multi-cultural people of the Middle East. Most assuredly our "Wise Men" took with them from the birthplace of Jesus the accounts of the "Baby King" to several parts of the world and influenced many non-Christian religions. Jesus became the antecedent for legends around the world. The Magi also prepared the ground for much of Jesus' ministry abroad during His lifetime. The visits of Jesus were heralded by many cultures as the answer to their own prophecies. We can only imagine the celebrations held when Jesus landed on foreign shores and was recognized by the locals. The few texts that describe those celebrations indicate that the life of Jesus was no mystery to the world.

Many of the eastern religious holy men were required by their separate faiths to pilgrimage their beliefs beyond their own borders. The origins of our modern concept of the "Pilgrimage" had long existed among religions that had to travel to see the real time events of their own prophesies unfold. It is amazing how influential the birth of a King of Israel was among the traditions of foreign lands at the time. The Wise Men were of different faiths and countries, but traveled together because of their shared beliefs in prophecy. None of them ever became Christians.

There were many groups of people have who looked forward to the occasional visits of "Wise Men." To be included in such a holy group, each member was usually of royal birth and had some sort of prominent religious insight and position. Each of them was an astrologer of sorts. That is why these men are sometimes referred to as Holy Wise Men and sometimes as Magi Kings. Of course, you would send a member of the "Royal House" to search for such an anticipated King. They also carried with them a king's ransom as a gift to such an important person. The king's ransom given by the Magi to Jesus at His birth would have made 100 families rich at that time.

There were extended royal families within a variety of countries, like Egypt, Persia, India, Palestine and even Rome itself, and they were often referred to as "Rulers," "Kings," or even Caesars, but were not themselves the actual heads of state - much like there are today in Europe and the Middle East. Constantine himself could trace his ancestor's back to the royal house of David, the Royal Family of Jesus.

Many modern scholars have presumed that all three Magi came from the ancient territory of Babylon, which conquered Palestine 600 years before the birth of Jesus. Jesus' royal ancestors escaped that massacre by fleeing to ancient England at that time. There were many small groups who escaped the slaughters of the Babylonians in 600 BC, which is a year far more critical to the world than we have heretofore imagined. There is little doubt that the Babylonians would have known "first hand" about the prophecies of the expected "King in Israel," because they had learned the tales from the Hebrews. It is also assured that they would have killed His ancestors had they known where they were, because they were the heirs to the throne of David and a royal bloodline. England was a very good hiding place for the high profile heirs to the throne of David. No wonder the ancestry of Jesus is so intertwined with the history of England. However, these three men, though they had traveled from their most recent stop in Babylon, originated from different countries. Research by the 15th century had identified these men and had rediscovered and recorded their names and homelands.

One of these Magi was of a much darker skin and probably from India, as the records have suggested. The fact that this one Magi was of an obviously different race gives us evidence that these kings were from different families and religious backgrounds. These three men were united in the search for the King of the Jews from their separate beliefs and traditions.

India later played a very important role in the mortal life of Jesus and also in the preservation of Christian scripture and prophecy. This particular Magi prepared his people in India for the eventual visit of the mortal Jesus to his own country just a few years later. Thus when Jesus arrived in Nepal, the people had already heard of his birth. Perhaps this is why Jesus is quoted in the holy books of the Hindu and recorded in the paintings and stained glass windows, sitting in traditional Hindu-like meditation, rather than being treated like a total outsider. Jesus' visit to India was just one of the forgotten travels of Christ between the ages of 14 and His final ministry. The tales of the mortal visit of Jesus to India are common in the streets there to this day.

There are several recent books about the visit of Jesus to Nepal; however, these books don't give a reason or a method for Jesus' appearance there. Jesus had sailed there on a ship of His great uncle, Joseph of Arimathea, as they were delivering metal from their mines in England. The ministry of Jesus was often associated with the delivery of metal products from the family owned mines.

Returning to these Wise Men, they often settled local disputes in their travels and were well respected by the governing bodies of many countries, including Rome. Such groups, like the Magi, were regular visitors in Palestine, the crossroads for merchants coming from the "East." The "East" had literally been a "Mecca" of religious wisdom, and their learned men had known about the prophesied "Messiah of Israel" as well as the Jews did themselves - maybe even better because of the ban on extra-Biblical writings in the Jewish synagogues from the time of the Macabeans.

The diverse ancient world of Jesus was a far more religious family/community than exists today. Certainly the birth of Jesus was not a local "myth" which sprang out of a single group of people, at a specific instant in history, as some faithless scholars/critics of Christendom now claim. A local myth doesn't just appear independently at a specific time in history among many cultures at the same time.

There is little doubt that the entire Eastern Province was aware of the Nazarene born in Bethlehem, as the prophecy had foretold, especially when Herod killed all their babies two years old and under in and around Bethlehem. Such a brutal act would not have gone unnoticed by the Jews, nor by anyone in the known world for that matter. News traveled faster in the world of Jesus than we think it did. There was a great expectancy among the people of Israel, and in many other countries, as they focused their eyes on Palestine and the baby Jesus - and then lost Him in their own midst until He was grown.

No wonder Caesar had sent a member of his own family to watch for this one man that could "trigger" more rebellion in his Eastern Province than any military group at the time. It is likely that Caesar feared not only for his Eastern Province, but also for much more of his territory, after the Magi Kings of the East broke the story to Herod about the birth of the prophesied Messiah.

This was not a casual visit of a wandering band of rich royalty who saw some bizarre celestial event. The visit of the Magi clarifies the fact that Jesus' coming was a long prophesied event among many countries and religions, and ultimately a critical part of the destiny of the entire world. We have long passed over the importance of the Magi because they force us to view the appearance of Jesus from a global perspective. The civilized churches of the world have been uncomfortable in sharing this saga of Jesus with the rest of the religious world. However, a clear understanding of Jesus is possible only for those who can look past their protected domain and canon and see Jesus for who He truly was and is - the Messiah of the entire world.

THE STAR OF BETHLEHEM

It is helpful to understand a little about the Star of Bethlehem when we refer to the Magi. If the Magi were anything, they were astronomers of the finest quality. Astronomy and prophecy bound these men together like brothers of the same flesh, though they were anything but that. Prophecy was often spoken in terms of astronomical events. The reason they came to the birthplace of Jesus was because they were "tipped off" to do so by the appearance of the star that was contained within their shared prophecy.

Answers to the questions, "What was this new star in the heavens? When did it appear? and why did it go away?" have baffled scholars since Jesus' birth. This star is really not as mysterious as we have been led to believe.

We can pinpoint the star of Bethlehem with a little look into prophecy, history and astronomical physics. For example, we know the exact day and year that Herod the King died. (Herod was the one who sought to kill the baby Jesus right after He was born.) Jesus was obviously born before the death of Herod, which was the result of a dreaded disease, on the night of a well-recorded eclipse of the moon in four BC. That date has never been in question and can be verified today. Some naive scholars feel that the celestial merger of Jupiter and Venus in two BC was the Star of Bethlehem; but that could not have been the case because

Herod was already dead by that time. Venus was the star of the Virgin. Perhaps we will find someday that "The Immaculate Conception," or the birth of the Virgin Mary, is associated with Venus.

Other modern scholars have searched the heavens for a nova, or a super nova, or any other recorded celestial anomaly that would have either been recorded in history, or could be retraced through computer recreations of the heavens at the time of the Jesus' birth. But none of these efforts has proved helpful.

The Chinese recorded seeing a comet in the sky in five BC, which lasted several weeks and covered about a quarter of the heavens from horizon to horizon. Scholars of the modern era have been excited over this discovery, thinking that this spectacular event could have been the Star of Bethlehem with its beautiful tail, like the one commonly pictured in Christmas art work. However, that comet appeared so close to the time of the death of Herod that it too could not have been the star for which we are looking.

The birth of Christ occurred during the time of a Roman census that was completed before the death of Herod. The Holy Family was required to return to their ancestral home to be taxed and counted in Bethlehem. Since that process took a couple of years to complete, it adds more time to the death of Herod in four BC - and also the birth of Jesus.

In addition, it is clear from the *Childhood Stories of Jesus* that the Holy Family remained in Egypt for a couple of years or so before they returned to their home in the city later named Nazareth after the death of Herod. There wasn't a city called Nazareth during Jesus' time. Therefore, we can add four years BC to two or three more, and the birth of Jesus had to have occurred around seven BC. Our modern calendars are off by seven years, which is coincidentally the same amount of time that they err in the birth of Christ and the age of Jesus himself when He died.

A Scythian monk, Dionysius Egnacius, who pieced together our calendar backward from the year AD 533, created the calendar we use today. He obviously missed by seven years. It was his assumption that Jesus was born in the year zero and died in 33 AD. He was originally commissioned by Caesar to create a calendar beginning with the first year of the Roman Empire. However, the year of the birth of Jesus was every bit as palatable to the Romans by that point.

If the scholars of today had turned to prophecy for the identity to the Star of Bethlehem to begin with, the problem would have been solved long ago. To get an accurate date for the birth of Jesus, we turn to the ancient prophets Daniel, the Jewish Rabbinical writer Abarbanel, and most important of all, the prophet Micah, for the answer. These texts are not in the Bible either.

Josephus, the Jewish traitor, said that there had been a "sign in the heavens" proclaiming the birth of the Jewish King. This is important only to the extent that it verifies that the Romans clearly knew the events surrounding the Savior's birth because Josephus wrote his histories at tables of the Roman Caesars.

The correct year of the birth of Jesus can also be determined from the stars, which have often been used to determine the years of other special events. There were ancient prophecies that accurately predicted future events. There was a merger of Jupiter and Saturn as they appeared in the constellation of Pisces three times in the year seven

BC. Our computer recreations can track these events today. Jupiter was well known from prophecy as the "Kingly Star," and Saturn was well known to them as the "Protector of Israel" for the same reason. The constellation of Pisces was to be the ancient prophesied location in the heavens where the sign of the Messiah would appear. So when the Star of the King merged with the Protector of Israel in the location of the Messiah's birth, the Magi came to search for the birth of the Messiah King of Israel. It was that simple. The symbol of the fish (Pisces) was used to denote Christianity in the early years in similitude of the birth of Jesus.

Kepler, who knew the correct identity of the Star of Bethlehem in the year 1603, said (as he watched the same celestial event occur once again) "As the two stars merged, they seemed to come closer together until all I could see in the sky was one bright star of wonderful brilliance." This merger of Jupiter and Saturn in Pisces has never again occurred three times in one year.

Matthew 2: 1-2 says, "Now when Jesus was born in Bethlehem of Judea in the days of Herod the King, behold there came Wise Men from the East to Jerusalem, saying, 'Where is He that is born king of the Jews. For we have seen His star in the East and we have come to worship Him.'" The words, "We have seen His star in the East" can be more correctly translated, "We have seen His star in the early dawn." The wise men didn't say they had seen His star "from" the East, they said they had seen His star "in" the morning sky.

In February, seven BC, the ancient astronomers watched the morning heavens as Jupiter moved into the constellation of Pisces and towards Saturn. The merger of

36

the two planets almost happened at that time, but did not. The entire astrological world was alerted to the events taking place in the sky, and there is evidence that a large number of them placed themselves on stand-by alert. These astronomers were already searching the skies for the sign because it was time for the fulfillment of the prophecies of Daniel and Micah.

The first time the merger actually occurred in seven BC was at daybreak on April 12th. However, the sun was also located in the constellation of Pisces on that day, and there wasn't as clear a view of the new star as there was twice later in the year. When Magi saw this event, they packed their traveling luggage and headed toward Palestine to meet the prophesied Messiah King of Israel. Some have asked why were they interested in the King of Israel to begin with if they were not Jewish? The answer was that they were interested in the King of Israel because they felt themselves part of the Messiah experience from their own religious traditions.

The new star guided them to the birthplace of Jesus because of its association with prophecy and not because it hovered over the manger containing the baby Jesus. How could someone find a manger, or a cave (the real birthplace of Jesus), in a foreign country by traveling to the point directly beneath a star that appears to be rotating around the earth? The stars do appear to travel from east to west in the sky as the earth turns, which may account for the Magi's comments that they followed the movement of the star to the birthplace of the Messiah. The Magi themselves questioned the residents of Bethlehem, and the emissaries of Herod, which obviously meant that the star didn't hover directly over some manger. Their prophecies indicated which town to go to, but that was it.

"The message of the stars was so powerful that no astrologer could ignore it." (*Did the Virgin Mary Live and Die in England?*, pg. 5) When the Magi visited Jesus, Jupiter and Saturn were a vision in the morning sky. The rays of the rising sun obscured the other stars, but they themselves were visible. This is important because the Magi themselves said that when the star of Bethlehem appeared, the other stars in the heavens were obscured in the sky. The only mystery left is which day of the two remaining mergers did the Magi arrive in Bethlehem?

The next time Jupiter and Saturn collided in the heavens was on May 29, when the constellation and the new star were visible for two hours. This gave the Magi nearly two months to complete their journey to Bethlehem, which was possible, and still was not enough time for the Holy Family to have returned to their home in pre-Nazareth after the traditional family reunions were over. This leads us to believe that Jesus was born in the first few days of April in seven BC. The Magi caught up to the baby Jesus in late May. The Star of Bethlehem heralded the birth of Jesus, but it took weeks for the Magi to complete their journey. The last time the two planets merged was on December 4 of the same year and was referred to in the aftermath of the Savior's birth in other records. What a rare event to have this same merger of Jupiter and Saturn three times in one year!

The fact that Jesus was born in seven BC gives credence to the modern beliefs that Jesus died at the age of 40 and not 33. Jesus may have died in 33 AD, but He most certainly was not 33 years old at that time. Jesus would have been 40 in the year 33 AD. That is very important for another reason. Forty is a particularly holy number for the Jews, who are among the most ardent followers of prophetic numerology. Forty was also the prophesied age of the Messiah at His demise.

Forty is ten times four. For the Jews the number ten represents the measure of responsibility for both God and man. Remember there were Ten Commandments. The number four represents that which is universal and also sets forth the full measure for probation and testing for the ancient Hebrews. The number 40 is used as a prophetic allusion to the coming of the Messiah. The rain fell on Noah for 40 days and nights, and Noah waited 40 days on dry land before he left the ark. Moses was 40 when he fled from Egypt. Moses was 40 when he left Egypt, 40 years more, when he delivered his people from the Egyptians. Moses was 40 additional years wandering in the wilderness. For 40 days Jesus remained on the earth and taught His disciples after His death. Saul reigned for 40 years. David reigned 40 years. Solomon reigned 40 years. Jesus fasted and was tempted 40 days in the wilderness. Nineveh was given 40 days to repent at the time of Jonah and the whale. The number 40 plays a prominent role in the recorded prophecies about the age of the Messiahs to come. Nothing about the number 33 is important for the Jews. However, 40 is the time period which identifies Jesus in Jewish eyes with many events in their faith, including the ones surrounding the coming of their Messiah.

THE TRAVELING JESUS

The mystery continues to this day about the actual life of Jesus that had made this famous baby a stranger to His own people when He grew up. How does one hide a Messiah in the midst of His own people? The answer lies somewhere along with the reason Jesus was taxed as a foreigner in His own country three years before His crucifixion? If Jesus had spent His whole life in Pre-Nazareth, why didn't the Jews recognize Him after all the sensational events that surrounded His birth and His family for years? Why didn't His people gather around this former "Baby King" instead of calling for His crucifixion in the streets of Jerusalem? The answer is clearly that Jesus was not in Palestine for the majority of His life. Jesus was traveling the world on the ships of His Great Uncle, Joseph of Arimathea, performing a ministry that is still a secret to those who profess to be Christian.

When Jesus began His final ministry among His own people, three years before His death, He was a stranger in town despite His wealth and miraculous birth. John the Baptist didn't even recognize Jesus at the family reunion on the day of feasting upon Jesus' arrival in Palestine. If anyone would have recognized Jesus, one would think that the man who had preached Jesus' virtues in the desert would have recognized Him. Jesus must have been abroad a long time. What ministry had Jesus been performing all this time that had kept Him from the eyes of His home country?

It is totally illogical to think that He had been working as a poor carpenter making wooden fences or pales with His father and then suddenly came out of obscurity to be the Savior of the world, our modern Christian traditional story. There are many who think that Jesus Himself didn't understand His own ministries until later in His life. The gift of the miraculous didn't suddenly begin at the age of 30 to dazzle the world for the next 100 generations.

Somewhere in the dusty past, modern Christians have lost the biography of the traveling Jesus that had taken Him completely out of the Near East. There are many countries that possess first-century legends of a man who healed the sick, raised the dead, walked on water, promised He would come again, was an olive skinned man with reddish tints in His hair and "ocean colored" eyes. These countries include England, India, Southern Africa, Australia, the Pacific Islands, the Far East, Greenland, and the Ancient Americas. That claim will sound absurd to most modern Christians, though their own traditions are equally anemic and enigmatic. However, we are just beginning to trace the legends of the travels of Jesus.

The anthropologists have been wrong in their presumption that the people of Jesus' time didn't have the facility to traverse the earth especially when it came to boats. At the time of Jesus a boat could travel 40 times further in one day than a camel. When we understand that the great uncle of Jesus owned merchant vessels and was the acting head of Jesus' family, everything falls into place.

Just ask the Brazilians who have found the wreckage off their coast of Roman merchant ships from the first century. Just ask the archeologists about the 2500 B. C. Pharaohs who were using cocaine and tobacco from the Americas. They found cocaine in the toxicological reports on their hair, and tobacco that had been used as an embalming agent. The herbalists from all over the world have attempted to find a native plant from Africa to justify that discovery, but have had no success. If the ancient Egyptians had access to products from the Americas, certainly the merchant ships from the time of Jesus did as well. That discovery was featured on one of the TV educational channels in a program called *The Curse of the Cocaine Mummy*. The examples of verified early global travel are too numerous to mention in this work. Our assumption that Columbus was the first to sail the Atlantic have long been debunked as a falsehood.

Just think for a minute. A man who could walk on the water and calm the very tempest could probably navigate the oceans, especially if His family owned the boats. Maybe there were many "chosen people" besides the Jews who had an intimate relationship with the Son of God. Maybe being the "original chosen people" was not such a distinction after all. Perhaps Jesus needed to visit them all. Could it be that everyone is a member of the fraternity of the Children of God after all?

SETTING THE STAGE

THE SECRET THAT COST JESUS HIS LIFE

During the last three years of Jesus' life, His fame, reputation, and ministry grew to the point that there was serious doubt that anything could have stopped the spread of His popularity. His supporters had reached even inside the Jewish Sanhedrin and Rome itself. There had been serious debate on the Sanhedrin council floor about the integration of Jesus and His teachings into Jewish tradition. Joseph of Arimathea and Nicodemus sponsored this debate. Each of the members of the Sanhedrin knew the oral traditions of the "Messiah Ben Judah" to be born "in the Meridian of Time," and each had a decision to make as to whether or not Jesus was, in fact, that man. In fact, the majority of the Sanhedrin already supported Jesus and had voted to accept Him when their fellow councilmen, Nicodemus and Joseph of Arimathea, made the proposal three years before the Crucifixion. These two men were enormously influential. In addition, there are several histories written by converted Roman military personnel that carried this message around the world. There were members of the Roman legends that became Christians before the death of Jesus, as well as just after the Crucifixion. Claudia Procula, the wife of Pilate, had already converted to Judaism by the time of the Crucifixion. If Procula were allowed to investigate the miracles of Jesus, certainly the Roman legions in Palestine would have been shown a level of tolerance as well.

The world changed suddenly when the enemies of Jesus found the one missing key that would allow them to be rid of Him permanently. That missing key was a hideous secret that Pilate kept from both his wife and Caesar. Pilate, the Governor of the Eastern Province of Rome, had been associated with Lucius Aelius Sejanus, a Roman noble in a secret feeble plot to kill his wife's grandfather, Tiberius Caesar. Lucius was, in fact, the patron of Pilate. Lucius was the praetorium prefect of Tiberius Caesar. It was Lucius that had taken Pilate out of the great schools of England and brought him to Rome. A "Prefect" was empowered to act for a ruler in his stead. Lucius had introduced Pilate to the majority of the Roman aristocracy and was thus his "Patron."

Lucius shared the rule of Rome with Tiberius Caesar and was handling the daily administration of Rome while Tiberius was "dominating the isle of Capri," on an "extended vacation" in his opulent home. Tiberius liked the trappings of the head of state, but preferred to let his Prefect act in his stead most of the time. This failed coup attempt had nothing to do with the death of Jesus...OR DID IT? Lucius was killed in 31 AD when his treachery was discovered. Pilate shared his fate not long afterwards. However, Pilate did not die for his part in the assassination attempt, but rather for his part in the crucifixion of Jesus. After the failed coup attempt Tiberius gathered all his suitors to Capri so that he could watch them. We know that Caligula, the successor of Tiberius, was summoned to Capri almost as a prisoner in 31 AD. Tiberius grilled Caligula with temptations for years because of Lucius' attempt on his life. After the failed coup attempt, Tiberius was nervous about everyone around him, especially those who could ascend to power after his death.

Like most plots that involve traitorous partners, the secret of the assassination plot had been leaked to Pilate's traitorous subjects, Herod, Caiaphas (the Chief Priest of the Sanhedrin), and Caiaphas's father-in-law, Annas (the former Chief Priest of the Sanhedrin). At this moment in history the greatest blackmail scheme of them all was born. The Sadducees of the Sanhedrin, and the paranoid Herod, had long thirsted for the blood of Jesus. The Pharisees and Essenes never thirsted after the blood of Jesus, though they may have annoyed Jesus from time-to-time. These three men preferred powerful and wealthy rule of Rome, rather than have in the country a Messiah King who was changing everything. They needed Jesus to disappear before their traditional beliefs, their political and religious power disappeared with them. It is critical to note that these three men were ardent allies of Rome, unlike the rest of the Jews outside the Sadducean political sect.

These three men used the blackmail information that they possessed on Pilate to coerce him to have Jesus crucified. There isn't a story, Biblical or not, that portrays Pilate as a willing participant in the death of Jesus. Now, we have a better understanding of why Pilate buckled under the pressure of the Sadducees and allowed Him to be crucified. Pilate was simply afraid of these three men who knew too much. This blackmail has long filled the Roman histories of the period, but we have refused to make the connection in public because it would alter tradition.

45

JESUS WAS NOT A SECRET AFTER ALL

The tremendous emergence of Jesus' ministry was no secret to the hundreds of thousands who had followed the legends of Jesus from before He was born. How do you keep the story of the angelic life of Mary, her heaven-chosen husband Joseph, and the birth of the Savior, that was heralded by foreign royalty, secret from the people? Obviously it was no secret at all. Jesus and His family were the rightful heirs to the throne of King David and were a highly respected and wealthy family. They held property in England, Egypt and in other countries throughout the world. When the occasional barbarian had historically conquered Palestine in the centuries before Christ, the royal family had to flee in exile to other countries, as did the family of Jesus. The country that most frequently became their home in exile was ancient England. The ancestors of Jesus may have lived abroad, but they retained their identity and ties to Palestine. Jesus' grandmother reverse immigrated prior to the birth of the Virgin Mary to get married to Joachim, a member of her own faith. Jesus' family was no stranger to England by the time He was born. This family had been chosen for the Messiah's birth, and everyone who was anyone knew it, though the family may not have continually lived in Palestine.

When Herod the King murdered Zacharias in the temple, just after the birth of Jesus, he had mistaken Jesus' newly born cousin, John the Baptist, for the prophesied baby "King of Israel." Herod had thought that the Messiah King would be the son of a high priest in the temple; so he had identified the correct family, just not the right person. Most everyone knew who the family of the Messiah would be. Zacharias was married to the Virgin Mary's cousin, Elizabeth.

Over the course of Jesus' lifetime there were multitudes that had pieced the puzzle together and had recognized Jesus for who He was, especially in Galilee where the family of Jesus was the most prominent. Perhaps Galilee kept the Holy Family incognito, rather than placing them as a large target for assassination in the religious center of Jerusalem.

Jesus Biblically fed thousands of "tag alongs" in Galilee with a few loafs of bread and a couple of fishes on two occasions during the last three years of His life. These few thousand "tag alongs" were just the tip of a much larger Christian "iceberg." The fact that Jesus had thousands of "tag along" disciples, at any given point in time, must have struck fear in the heart of Herod and the Sadducean allies of Rome. Jesus was not as well respected in Jerusalem the real ancestral home of the Jews. In a sense, Jesus was considered a rich kid from the "wrong side of the tracks" in Jerusalem by the time He was an adult.

If Herod had been more in touch with the common people of Galilee, where he had his palatial residence, he would have heard about Mary's son. Before Jesus was born, Mary had been sequestered in the great temple of Jerusalem to protect her from scandal for 12 years of her life. Her "Virgin Birth" was well known, from the time she was a child. Perhaps Herod hadn't recognized Mary because she grew up hidden in the temple in Jerusalem to the south, away from the actual home of Herod Antipas. Since Herod was not invited into the temple because of his wickedness, the temple may have been the best hiding place for the Virgin Mary. Remember that it was Zacharias who was murdered by this Herod. It was the custom at that time to sequester virgins from rich families in the temple. Mary, however, was special. We know that there were some attempts made to buy Mary from the temple by those who knew of her royal birthright and progeny-to-be. Albiathar was one of those rich, proud fathers who wanted a royal mate for his son and tried to attract the attentions of Mary.

It was the high priest, Zacharias, who had entered Mary's room in the temple with food each day and often found the angels had already fed her. Perhaps Zacharias' early involvement with his much younger cousin Mary was one of the reasons for Herod's confusion over Zacharias and which of the many babies should be killed in Herod's pursuit of the Prophesied Baby. Joseph was not yet Mary's husband; thus were no fathers to be questioned by Herod in the pursuit of the Holy Baby, except Mary's family relationship with Zacharias. Zacharias was no stranger to Herod, who knew that at least one famous baby, John the Baptist, had just been born and heralded by the people in the streets. Herod killed Zacharias between the altar of the temple and the front door, looking for the Baby King. The wilderness was eventually the perfect hiding place for John the Baptist who needed to live incognito. The birth of John the Baptist, six months before Jesus, was a most excellent diversion and protection for the actual birth of Jesus. Herod could have easily searched for Jesus in Egypt had he known that's where they were.

Joseph escaped out the "back door" of Judea with his future wife and the baby Jesus to Egypt, a country that was not unfamiliar to the family of Joseph and Mary because her uncle, Joseph of Arimathea, was born there in Marorica Egypt. Some of the spectacular events that happened to the Holy Family in Egypt are highlighted in the first book in the Hidden Treasure series, *The Hidden story of Jesus' Childhood.*

We have been left with the impression from the Bible that most of the people in Palestine either didn't know about Jesus, or that they disliked Him because of the reported outcry of the Jews to kill Jesus in Jerusalem the day of His crucifixion. Once again the Biblical tradition leads us astray. In reality the majority of the people liked Jesus, whether they believed in His divinity or not. Who wouldn't like a sweet spirited man who could heal the sick and who spoke directly to the hearts of the people of eternal peace for all the children of God? Who wouldn't love a man who loved their children more than the aristocracy and any earthly title and position they had tried to thrust upon Him? Who wouldn't love a man who liberally gave of the money of His family to the poor and preached the gospel among the lowly of the land? Who, in that time, wouldn't have followed the events of a man from a wealthy family to begin with, who later ate with the publicans and sinners in the common houses of the streets?

For those who wanted to be free from the tyranny of Rome, Jesus was that Messiah King who could free them from their political oppressors. The oral traditions swept through the streets, though they were disallowed in the temples. There were many that became disappointed and confused, over the true identity of Jesus when He didn't mount a military insurrection against the Romans during His lifetime. Perhaps this was the source of some of their anger, as the Jews had felt that when the Messiah came, He would save their earthly lives. They had not understood that the Messiah had come to save their immortal souls as the prophecy had intimated. They had confused His Second Coming at the end of the earth with His mortal presence in the "meridian of time." You can't blame them. They had been a conquered people for so long that they thirsted for freedom.

The somewhat illiterate masses had been mystified by their own prophesies that spoke of a "Messiah Ben Judah" who would be killed on a cross for the sins of His own people. The Jews didn't like to think of themselves as a sinful population that needed a Savior for their souls. Today the Jews do not even acknowledge the existence of a soul at all. They were the "chosen people" in their own minds and that made them right. The entire prophecy sounded strange in their ears.

THE PROPHESIED METHOD OF JESUS' DEATH

The method of His prophesied death also sounded strange to the Jews. The Jewish procedure for executing capital punishment had long been stoning or strangulation. The prophesied crucifixion of the Messiah was a Roman system of capital punishment and the Jews, who were a newly conquered people, had just recently been exposed to this type of death. There were some that remembered their own ancient prophecy and had privately warned Jesus about the Romans and their crucifixion style of execution. Strangely these people who were warning Jesus were Pharisees, who have been wrongfully blamed for His death. The Jews especially didn't like the part of the prophecy that said that the Messiah's own people would reject Him. That wouldn't have made very good "dinner conversation" for a people who prided themselves in their heritage, obedience and piety.

The Sadducees, however, would have used or abused anyone or anything in order to protect themselves from the change in their lives that a Messiah represented. When they looked for a "patsy" to work their evil for them, they found Pilate and a dirty piece of blackmail. Pilate was a strong and decisive character in history, but the Sadducees had found his "Achilles heel." Little did Pilate know that he was doomed if he protected Jesus and doomed if he didn't? Christianity and Judaism were doomed to be permanently separated when Pilate found himself trapped by his dark personal secret.

To the Sadducees, Jesus was the greatest threat to traditional Judaism that they had ever known. The Jews had been a conquered people before, but none of the conquerors had had the power to destroy their traditional way of life from within. During the last three years of Jesus' life, the Jews were rapidly approaching a major transition in their own faith, and the "good old boys" in power didn't like it at all.

The Sadducees found it politically and spiritually unwise to simply murder Jesus. Certainly the Sadducees could have requested that Herod "do the deed." Though the Sadducees and the Herod Dynasty had their differences, they were both Jewish political allies of Rome, unlike the majority of the rest of the Jews including the Pharisees. The Sadducees held the leadership of the Sanhedrin and had a broad range of autonomy because of their political support of Rome.

Herod had the power, under the rule of Rome, to execute any non-Roman he chose. However, in the minds of the Sadducees even Herod was too close to Jesus to be linked with His death. Had Herod executed such a popular figure, there may have been a "backlash" that might very well have endangered Sadducean authority and the Herod Dynasty. The Sadducees needed someone non-Jewish to do it for them. There was still a commandment from the tablets of Moses against murder. That may not have impressed Herod, who had murdered thousands, but it most certainly influenced the Sadducees who envisioned themselves holy men of God. The Sadducees had long walked the fine line between obedience to the letter of the law and the spirit of their own teachings. The obvious choice for the Sadducees was to have Rome get rid of Jesus for them. When they stumbled onto the blackmail information on Pilate, they knew they had Jesus where they wanted Him. The excuse the Sadducees used to condemn Jesus was that He had said He could destroy the temple and then raise it in three days. That was insurrection against the Romans and had nothing to do with Jewish law.

SOMETHING STRANGE WAS HAPPENING
TO PILATE

Pilate had been well trained in the "Roman Way" of settling disputes. He had seen it in Rome and had used it many times himself. "Governor Pilate" frequently had to settle matters of civil disobedience and condemn men to death. It was the strangest of behaviors to see this strong leader wash his hands of something that might result in more Jewish insurrection. The "washing of the hands" was not an act of a traditional Roman Governor, but a well-known tradition among the Jews. Why would a Roman Governor who had already shed the blood of many Jews use a Jewish tradition to proclaim his innocence from the blood of this Jew? We need to turn to his wife for the answer to that question.

Something strange was going on behind the scenes when Pilate wiped his laundered hands on a towel and refused to deal with the one event that had the potential to incite every man, women, and child in Judea. Pilate knew, and so did most of the leaders of Judea, that the handling of the "Messiah matter" was a classic case of the kind of dispute he was first sent from Rome to oversee. Surely Pilate knew that Jesus was probably the very "King of the Jews" that he had been sent to find and control.

Like most blackmail schemes, the payment didn't stop the horror for Pilate, who later paid the blackmail ransom in full. It was the fact that Pilate allowed Jesus to be crucified that cost him his life. It was Tiberius Caesar that handed the head of Pilate on a platter to his wife for ironically allowing Jesus to be crucified. "Hold on!" some might say. "You mean Tiberius Caesar didn't want Jesus to be crucified?"

There was something even stranger going on when later we see Pontius Pilate and his wife, Claudia Procula, remembered alongside Christian Saints by factions of the early Christian churches. Today Pilate is still viewed as an "innocent and virtuous figure" by the Roman church. He is not only vindicated, but is so Christianized that he passes into Christian Byzantine legend as a Saint. He is still celebrated today as a "martyr" in the Coptic Christian church. We are forced to ask ourselves, "Where is that story." The names of Pilate and Claudia Procula appeared on the calendar of venerated days in infant Christianity. The early Christians even renamed two of their holy mountains after Pilate. Why would the Christians remember Pilate alongside their Saints? Have we forgotten or misplaced the real Pilate?

CLAUDIA PROCULA, PILATE'S WIFE

The wife of Pilate was the one sweet Roman voice in the whole tragedy of Jesus. Though she had been Roman by birth, she later converted to Judaism and was just becoming a fledgling disciple of Jesus, as were many of the wives of powerful Judean leaders, including those in the Sanhedrin itself. Jesus had been gathering a following from some very unexpected places during the last three years of His life. However, many of these people hadn't quite made the transition to full-fledged disciples by the time of His death. The resurrection of Jesus triggered the conversion of many, including Procula and then Pilate himself.

Procula was among those who followed the constant neighborhood commotion of healings and sweet messages from a "God/Man" who respected women. She may have progressed more quickly in her conversion, but Jesus lived north in Galilee and only infrequently visited Jerusalem, the home of Pilate, because Jerusalem was the enemy of Jesus. By the time of Jesus, there had been bloodshed for 300 years of civil war between Jerusalem and Galilee. There had been lingering bitterness between the residents of Galilee and Jerusalem over the treatment of one of the princesses of Benjamin in Jerusalem by the marauders from the north in the third century BC. The Jews and the Romans viewed their women as property, and they didn't like outsiders

54

"messing" with their possessions. This civil war in Palestine was not the first war to be fought over a woman in history.

It always seemed to be the women who were first drawn by the strong emotions of spiritual awakening. In the case of Pilate, Procula led him to an awakening of his own that in the end became the most important thing in his life. If the women of Judea had been in control of those fateful events, things may have turned out very differently.

Procula was one of the favorites of the Roman Caesars and had influence throughout Rome. From all accounts she was a most pleasant and beautiful person. Procula was the "silver spoon" in her husband's mouth and also the love of his life. Surely by the time Jesus was brought to trial, Pilate had heard about him many times from his wife and from a variety of other contemporaries as well. Pilate had even seen some Jewish traditional practices in his home, as is evidenced by his use of Jewish traditional symbols at the death of Jesus. Someone was obviously teaching the new governor Pilate, about Jewish mannerisms.

In those times conversion to another faith was viewed very differently than it is today. Many of those converted to Christianity never saw such development within their personal belief as a conversion at all. The people of different lands often shared beliefs as logical extensions of one another. The wandering Magi from the eastern religions were a prime illustration of sharing prophesied beliefs about the Jews. The Magi ironically returned Jewish prophecy to the Jews themselves. The common origins of separate beliefs were far more palatable to the people of that time than in our own. Today Moslems, Jews, Christians and others as well, are worlds apart with high fences between them. Formerly, ancestral beliefs of these different people were sisters in the minds of many, as truly they should be today.

The majority of the world's religious practices have common origins and each of these common origins found a place for the Messiah within their own teachings. Many have conjectured how wonderful the world would be today if we could return to the family status that was shared by our common ancestors. Few know that there are prophecies that speak of returning to a common family once again.

THE DREAM OF PROCULA

The night before Jesus was brought to trial, Procula had a vision that warned her husband against harming Jesus. She told Pilate in no uncertain terms that if he were to harm Jesus, he would lose his own life as a result. This vision of Procula is referred to in several places in historical records. It would be exciting to have known more of the details. History records that Procula saw even more than just the death of her husband as a result of the death of Jesus. Though she didn't understand, she saw the chaos of a hundred generations because of the decision in her husband's hands. Coincidentally, and prophetically, a hundred generations brings us to our own day and the prophesied Second Coming of the Messiah. (Twenty years per generation times 100 is 2,000 years.)

The next time Jesus is to come, prophecy says He will finally (1) reign as King of Kings, (2) bring 1,000 years of world peace with Him, and (3) free all His people from oppression. That freedom will not be limited to just the Jews or the faithful Christians, but will be extended to all the children of God. That day of 1,000 years of peace should be a source of hope and dreams for our children's children.

Who among us wouldn't suffer that our children might be safe and happy? Who among us would tell our children only nightmares and not tell them about a time when dreams will come true? What malevolent instinct within us would use the fear of His coming as a weapon to separate men further, or for personal gain? Who among us would limit those to be caught up at His coming, when clearly there is hope for everyone?

The doctrines of fear and elitism have subjugated the masses and have caused contention among us far too long. We can understand the real events of His Coming only when we are willing to see all that He has already provided for us. All of God's children have books and records left to them by the Master Himself. Why would we think we are unique? Arrogance is the sin most often mentioned in the Bible itself and was the major theme of Jesus' teachings. He may have spent the last three years of His life in Palestine, but He certainly had sailed the world and had taught many cultures the message of love and peace before that time. Men have changed the books to read that they were the only special people. Truly we are all special. The miracle is that we all are special to Him.

There are scholars who from prophecy, have attempted to sequence each and every destructive event at the end of the world, and all the evil players, but have not even mentioned any of the events of the 1,000 years of peace that are to follow. Those events are far more important and will last much longer than the short cataclysm preceding them. The tragedy of man is that we have all followed one catastrophe after another, as if we chronicle our lives by the evil within them. Someday that will be different if we are to share the heavens with the heavenly. There will be a happy

57

ending to the world, but what is a happy ending without some pathos? After all, it is the pathos that will eternally punctuate the lessons of mortality. In the end mortality will appear more like a great learning experience than a test. The ones who will suffer most are the ones who refused to learn more.

The plot "thickens" when we discover that as Procula followed the life of Jesus in the streets of Judea, she reported to her grandfather Tiberius Caesar in letters regarding this God/Man who could heal with "a word from His mouth." Tiberius Caesar was personally interested in this "Jesus figure" because he had an affliction that could not be cured by the best medicines of that time. There was nothing Tiberius could buy with his money or could manipulate with his power, that could heal himself. Thus Tiberius wanted to believe his favored granddaughter when she spoke in her letters of the "Great Healer" in his Eastern Province. It was then that Tiberius Caesar sent a letter to Pilate commanding him to bring the "Healer Jesus" to Rome to perform a "Royal Healing." But the letter came too late for Pilate, who had already allowed Jesus to be crucified. It is interesting to note that the name Jesus means healer.

WHO WAS THIS SANHEDRIN THAT HAD SUCH POWER OVER PILATE?

The Sanhedrin was the ruling body of the Jews, which consisted of 70 members plus a Chief High Priest for a total of 71. The word Sanhedrin came from the Greek Sundering, meaning sitting in council. This Council of Seventy was an office of priesthood, organized by Moses, for the administration of both religion and government. The office of High Priest was not an exclusive title that belonged to one man alone. High Priest was a priesthood office that could be held by many men at one time, similar to the Christian priesthood office of Bishop. The Chief High Priest was the title given to the head of the Sanhedrin Council and retained by him even after he stepped down after one year, like a title emeritus. The term of office was for one year, but there are indications that some of them were renewed in their office and held the position longer. The Sanhedrin contained powerful factions within its structure. The first were the Sadducees.

THE SADDUCEES, THE RULING HIERARCHY

The Sadducees had made their peace with Rome, unlike the Pharisees or other Jewish groups like the Essenes who had buried the "Dead Sea Scrolls" at Qumran in their flight from Roman extermination. Although, the Sadducees were only a small part of the Sanhedrin, they were a small group of men who principally consisted of the ruling leaders of the Sanhedrin Council plus a handful of other orthodox Jews. As is the case in many religions, the most fanatical believers rise to leadership positions. Annas, and then Caiaphas, and later Ananias (the next Chief Priest and the son of Caiaphas) were Sadducees, and this family held the Chief High Priest position during the time of the crucifixion. It was the Sadducees who blackmailed Pilate into trying Jesus as a traitor, after they had failed to get the support of the majority of the Sanhedrin to condemn Jesus to death for other reasons.

This is the terrible secret of the version of the crucifixion from the Gospel of John. In the Gospel of John, the Sanhedrin had met two weeks prior to the crucifixion to decide the matter of Jesus not the night he was brought before Pilate. The vote of the Sanhedrin two weeks prior, had vindicated Jesus and had set him free to walk the streets. There are records that have indicated that the vote was 40 to 31 to acquit Jesus.

These extremely conservative Sadducees believed exclusively in the Torah which contained the five books of Moses and did not allow for the tremendous additional Jewish scripture and written by their own holy prophets. Most of the remnants of the prophecies that had been uttered by the rest of their 24 prophets still continued in oral tradition, though those written records were largely housed in other countries like Egypt and were forbidden in Jewish temples. There is little doubt that the Jews knew most of the stories of the Messiah through their oral conversations, but the writings, which contained the actual prophecies, were

60

banned from their synagogues. Ignoring scripture has always been a historical problem for Jews and Christians alike. The rejection of scripture and the refusal to recognize that neither the Torah nor the Bible was complete, has cost this world an era of peace. We are lucky that the countries of the Magi, among others, preserved some of the messages for us today. The world will be astounded when we retrieve from "strangers" our own prophecies from our own prophets. The East continues to hold a huge library of these documents that will shortly be in our hands. The Magi learned of Jesus from these libraries. Watch for the "Six Baskets" from the East. Watch for the opening of books that have been sealed for millennium. The 24 prophets were told by the heavens to seal and hide some of their writings. We are the generation that will benefit from them. Will we be willing to accept them when they come? The great published discoveries from Qumran and the banks of the Nile River are just the beginning.

The refusal to accept all the writings of ancient prophets cost the Jews the very Messiah they had been waiting for. Christians have no idea what their rejection of extra-Biblical holy writings has cost them. The Christians of today walk around with Jesus on their lips, but with rejection of the extra-Biblical stories of Jesus, just like many Jews did in Jesus' time. Reading material outside the Bible is considered "heresy" for Christians to this day. This is a very strange behavior for outsiders to observe, just like it was unfortunate that the Jews missed the very Messiah that they had waited so long to embrace.

There are those in every religious persuasion that like to stand alone and "wale" to the public while holding up the Bible, the Torah or the Koran, that they are the only

61

"chosen" of God. Paradoxically, God views us all as His prideful children and claims us all for His own.

There are Christians who preach to the world that God miraculously preserved His "word" for us today in the Bible, and yet they ignore everything He has preserved outside the Bible. Is it important which mortal group preserved the words of Jesus? Couldn't God have "miraculously" preserved His own words for us in His own way without vindicating one church, and rejecting the rest in the process?

THE SCRIPTURES

Let us put the scriptures into perspective for a moment. There were over 700,000 ancient scrolls destroyed in the fire of 63 B. C. at the sacred library of Alexandria, Egypt. The council of seven priests, representing the tribes of Israel, had chosen a compendium among those scrolls a decade before the fire, and it became known as the Old Testament. These 84 men had to travel outside their own country, like the Magi had to travel to visit the birth of Jesus, to find their own writings. Clearly there were many more sacred documents in that great library than we have in our possession today. However, 70 years after the fires had cooled was not enough time for the priests to have forgotten everything they knew about the coming of the Messiah. Their oral traditions preserved many things that the chanters no longer chant in our day. How far must we travel to find our own records written for today?

Most of us understand the dark politics after the crucifixion era that prevented the emerging Christian

Church from turning to "heathen powers" for their lost history and tradition. The Nicene Council, from which our Bible was derived, was evidence that the fight for scripture still raged 300 years after the death of Jesus. Arius, Bishop in Egypt, was telling the second and third generation Apostolic Fathers that they had left out critical sacred writings. Arius lost that battle in the Nicene Council and we settled for the Bible. That doesn't diminish the rightful claim of the Bible, but it does prove conclusively that the emerging Christians hadn't yet learned the lessons of the Jews.

There is still something very strange in the fact that the Old Testament of the Christians came out of Egypt and not Palestine. The broad story of Christianity is not complete unless we take into account the writings from Egypt which "showcased" the power of Jesus during His childhood. The baby Jesus was a sensation among the Egyptians. (See that story in the first book in this series, *Hidden Stories of the Childhood of Jesus*.) In addition, Egypt had harbored the records of the 24 prophets for thousands of years because the Jews wouldn't tolerate them all in their synagogues. The house of Israel had to travel to retrieve the Old Testament from the hands of "heathens" because they didn't have the books in their libraries. Tragically the Nicene Council ignored Egypt as a source for the New Testament. We know that at least Mark had for a long time studied in Egypt to become a Scribe. They even ignored the writings of Jesus' immediate family and sadly of Jesus Himself. We know that they wrote because the predecessor of the Bible itself was a book called *The Only Rule of Our Faith*, which contained the writings of the family of Jesus. This group of documents was carried around the ancient world like we carry the Bible today. None of those writings are in the Bible. Jesus said several times that in the end "That which was hidden will be made manifest." Those who don't tolerate more will miss it again.

THE PROBLEMS WITH THE GOSPELS

Both modern scholars and literary content specialists say that there is serious doubt that the versions of the Gospels of Matthew and Luke that we now possess were personally written by either Matthew or Luke. Our Biblical versions contain significant portions of the original Gospels, but they have definitely been altered as they were passed down through the oral traditions of first and second centuries.

Many extra-Biblical writings contrast with some of the simple details of Matthew and Luke, but vindicate the version of those same events contained within the Gospel of John. Most people are unaware of the fact that there are contradictions within the Bible itself, especially among the Gospels of Matthew, Mark, Luke, and the "eyewitness" Gospel of John. As was mentioned earlier, the extra-Biblical texts and the Gospel of John confirm the fact that Jesus appeared before the Sanhedrin two weeks prior to His crucifixion. In the Gospel of John, Jesus continues to walk the streets after His Sanhedrin trial, and the Extra-Biblical texts state that He was completely exonerated at that time. Jesus did not appear before the official body of the Sanhedrin the night before the crucifixion, as is suggested in Matthew and Luke. It was against Jewish law to have the Sanhedrin meet at night for any reason, and if the Jews could pride themselves in anything, it was their obedience to law. Surely they would have waited until the rising of the sun the following day rather than violate that strict tradition. The Sanhedrin valued the law more than the truth, and their traditions more than the reality of their own Messiah in their midst.

The world needs to know, that the Jewish Sanhedrin was not the body that condemned Jesus, nor at fault for His arrest and crucifixion. Jesus' arrest and trials the night before His crucifixion were the fault of the Sadducees alone. There were Pharisees present in the entourage of the evening, but they were often present when the Sadducees were doing their evil, like a counterbalance to keep the Sadducees from "running totally amuck." The Pharisees were truly concerned about the "affect of Jesus" on their money, which is reflected in their concerns of the evening about the destruction of the temple, but none of them called for the actual blood of Jesus. We see the same scenario repeated when Paul was on trial before King Herod Agrippa. The battle between the Sadducees and the Pharisees was played out once again on that occasion and is explained more clearly in Acts 23.

If we were to combine the Sadducees and the Pharisees together, they still didn't make up the majority of the Sanhedrin. The Sadducees are often mentioned in the Bible because they were the leaders of the Sanhedrin, and the Pharisees were mentioned because they were the very rich. Had the Essenes been present at the crucifixion events of Jesus we would have seen some fireworks in Jesus' defense, because they were ardent supporters of Christ. Jesus even wore the robes of the Nazarene - an off-shoot of the Essene movement. The Essenes were supporters of the common man.

The guilt for the crucifixion belongs to the Sadducees and Herod all by themselves. Many of the Pharisees were arrogant and defensive men and were often criticized by Jesus in the Bible, but they were not the instigators of the crucifixion. How much blood of the Jew has been spilt because we have universally blamed all the Jews for the death of Jesus? The official governing body of the Jews (the Sanhedrin) found Him innocent. How many lives would have been spared if the histories contained within the Bible had not been limited by tradition? How much confusion and divisiveness could have been avoided by simply accepting the extra-Biblical histories as something other than heresy?

In the "Pistas Sophia" Matthew and Luke, along with Thomas, were commissioned by the resurrected Jesus to set down His words in writing. We have the remnants of the Gospels of Matthew and Luke in the Bible, but the Gospel of Thomas was excluded, though clear texts have been discovered in our time. The Gospel of Thomas is one of the most important and easy to understand recitations of Jesus Himself in existence. We must remember that Thomas was the younger brother of Jesus and knew Him as no other. This Thomas was called Judas Didimus Thomas and was often referred to as the twin of Jesus because he looked so much like Him. Of course, he would look like Him because they shared the same mother.

The Gospel of John is unique because he was the only apostle personally present for the entire crucifixion. The Gospel of Mark is special because it preceded the Gospels of Matthew and Luke. Scholars say that it appears that the actual preservers of Matthew and Luke took many things from Mark to fill in the gaps in the Gospels of Matthew and

Luke. Mark was well respected in the first and second centuries because he had spent years of training in the prestigious schools in Alexandria, Egypt to be a Scribe. Once again, it is Egypt that is the hub of Christian scholarship. It is an old and common story. It was never the intent of Mark to have his Gospel used to fill in the gaps of other writers. Mark will be the subject of an additional book in this series because his Gospel was never fully recorded in the Bible. We do, however, have reputable copies of the second half of Mark in existence today.

How many more New Testament writings were housed in Egypt, like Arius contended at the Nicene Council? What other countries still possess documents that rightfully belong in the New Testament? We know that all the books by and about women were burned in huge fires around 200 A. D., more than a hundred years before the Nicene Council. We have clear copies of the Gospel of Mary Magdalene today. Her message for the world reflects the sweetness of the women in Jesus' life.

The fact that there is substantial evidence that the Gospels of Matthew and Luke have been changed by oral tradition has given rise to the broadly accepted concept of the "Q." The "Q" is thought to be the original notes and oral traditions, which pre-date our versions of the Gospels. No one has ever found a written copy of the "Q," but rhetorically it has been identified and traced through the early centuries after Christ. The "Q" after all is referring to oral tradition.

The Gospels of Matthew, Mark and Luke substantially mislead us in the birth of the Savior as well. Those stories are contained in the *Hidden Stories of the Childhood of Jesus*, the first book in this series. The real description of Joseph and Mary and their parents is missing from the Bible. The Immaculate Conception (the miraculous birth of the Virgin Mary) is missing from the Bible, though we still have that oral tradition with us today. The birthplace of Jesus in a cave just outside Bethlehem is missing from the Bible. If you go to Bethlehem today and ask to see the birthplace of Jesus, they usher you into a cave. The very siblings of Jesus are also excluded from the Bible. How could we know about the family of Moses and miss the brothers and sisters of Jesus?

Don't look too critically at the Jews or their Scribes. The evolving Christian churches have followed in their footsteps, making many of the same mistakes. Human beings, after all, suffer from mortal diseases that only God can remedy.

A great number of our extra-Biblical writings are ironically housed today in the extensive Codex Vanticanus, the privately guarded church libraries in Rome. Occasionally material escapes the Vatican today, but even when it does, our own ignorance and prejudices protect it from public acceptance and acclaim.

PHARISEES, THE MISUNDERSTOOD

The Pharisees were a far more interesting group of men, though they comprised only five to ten percent of the Jews. The Pharisees were politically liberal and religiously conservative, which combination is common for many of the wealthiest men in our day. The Pharisees consisted of the very wealthy Jews, which was probably the reason they comprised such a small percent of the people. It was the conservative and narrow-minded religious nature of the Pharisees that caused Jesus to condemn them in the New Testament. It was their liberal politics which drew the Pharisees to Paul when they attempted to help him during his own trial before Herod Agrippa, 20 plus years later.

The name Pharisee means "separatist." The Pharisees came from the Macabean movement, which attempted to build a fence around the Torah while barely tolerating other worldly views. In their narrow mindedness, they had ignored the blatant prophecies in their own midst about the coming of the Christ (Christ meaning "Anointed with Oil"), though they had talked about Him liberally among themselves and had chanted His traditions at their religious gatherings. The Pharisees had an elaborate system of oral traditions which made them the chanters and cantors of the Jews at that time. The Pharisees were popular and well respected among ordinary Jews for their sometimes-charitable natures and their extreme wealth.

The Pharisees saw Rome as oppressive, unlike their Sadducean counterparts. It is amazing how much wealth the Romans had left in the hands of the Pharisees after their conquest of Palestine. The Pharisees hated Rome because it represented a threat to their money - even more than a threat to their own people. Many of the rich Pharisees had sadly acquiesced to the idea that the Jews had been, and would continue to be, a conquered people for the foreseeable future. They tolerated the Sadducean alliances with Rome because the Sadducees peacefully allowed the Pharisees to retain their money and to conduct their business.

The Talmud says there were seven classes of Pharisees, only one which acted out of love. We should remember that one of the reasons that the Pharisees were so generally condemned by Jesus is that six of the factions were hate-filled people. Most of their behavior was motivated directly, or indirectly, by their wealth. However, we should also remember that one of those factions attempted to spare Jesus from the Romans, to integrate Him into Jewish tradition, to intercede in behalf of Paul before King Herod Agrippa, and to counter-balance the real evil from the Sadducees. That was a pretty large task.

IMPORTANT CHARACTERS AND THEIR ROLES

THE ROLE OF THE PHARISEES IN THE CRUCIFIXION

The Pharisees had privately warned Jesus about the wrath of Herod. It was also the Pharisees who requested of Pilate a guard for the tomb of Jesus so that the Sadducees would not throw Jesus' body into a "pit," as the Sadducees had intended. The Pharisees didn't want the Sadducees, or the Romans, to have exclusive control of the tomb. Controlling the tomb of Jesus was the only way to safeguard not only the body of Jesus, but to control the rumors of His prophesied resurrection to come.

The Pharisees could not have used the Sanhedrin Police Force, which was operating under the direction of the Sadducees during the trial and crucifixion of Jesus. A Sadducee guard at the tomb of Jesus would have guaranteed that the body of Jesus would have ended up in a pit. The Romans could not have exclusively controlled the guard, or the Sadducees would have used the "blackmail" to cause the body to end up in the pit as well. Pilate had washed his hands of the whole thing by that time anyway and didn't care where they buried Jesus. Most of the apostles had run away and didn't have the resources to guard the tomb either.

The only hope for neutrality was a Roman guard at the tomb under the control of the Pharisees, probably at the

71

request of Joseph of Arimathea and Nicodemus. That appears like a contradiction in terms, because the Pharisees hated Roman intervention in anything. However, Pilate eventually loaned the Pharisees a "few good men," at the request of the provincial Roman Senator Joseph of Arimathea, to counterman the Sadducean police force. It was the Sadducean Police Force that was the real threat to the tomb of Jesus to begin with and not the Roman army. The Romans would have had little reason to protect the dead body of Jesus because they didn't believe the rumors of the resurrection. The Romans were not accustomed to guarding the bodies of those whom they killed. The only reason for a guard came at the request of Joseph of Arimathea to protect the body of Jesus from the Sadducees. Once again the Pharisees were constantly attempting to compensate for the actions of the Sadducees.

Joseph of Arimathea, as the great uncle of Jesus, and as a provincial Senator of Rome, had certain rights to command an independent guard from Pilate. Joseph of Arimathea not only arranged for a guard at the tomb, but the tomb of Jesus was his own personal property, which further illustrates his involvement. Jesus was buried in a family tomb like most of our dead today. Joseph of Arimathea had acted as the father of Jesus since the death of Joseph when Jesus was about 14 or 15.

If the guard at Jesus' tomb had been under the direction of the Roman legion they would never have run away when the angel rolled away the stone at theresurrection. This would have been considered as desertion. Even falling asleep on guard, was tantamount to a brutal death sentence. A Roman guard would have at least reported the events to their Roman leaders, who in turn, would have come to investigate. The only report given by the guard at the tomb was the made to the rulers of the Synagogue, of which Joseph of Arimathea was a most prominent member. That report was intended for the ears of Joseph of Arimathea, who himself had been imprisoned by the Sadducees at that time. The guards simply came to report to him who had hired them.

We can tell a lot about the events of the crucifixion by who reported to whom. The Sadducean leaders had locked Joseph of Arimathea in a room "with no windows" to prevent his further interference with their plans. The Roman guard didn't understand that they had really reported to the enemy when they made their report to the Sadducean leaders of the Sanhedrin. After all the guards presumed, that Joseph of Arimathea was an ally of the Sadducean leaders of the Sanhedrin because they often saw them together and knew that they both sat on the same council. The Roman guard didn't know who the real enemy was.

It was the women in Jesus' life that found the tomb apparently deserted on the third day following the death of Jesus, when they came with their boiled "Easter Eggs" in a basket to properly prepare His body for permanent interment. The eggs were intended to feed the guards at the tomb and allow the women to do their job. The guards had simply run home after the angel rolled away the stone and before the women appeared on the scene. They appeared again a day or two later looking for Joseph of Arimathea to give their report.

We soon find that a great Christian movement was generated among the Roman military because of the events occurring at the death and resurrection of Jesus. After all, the soldiers were the ones that saw the miracles firsthand. Some of the guards wrote books about the life of Jesus, which books are not found in the Bible, but are prominent in history. There are those who thought that the writings of the Roman guards were "heresy" designed to destroy the church. However, no one who has read those documents fairly could conclude any such conspiracy. There was no reason for the Roman guard to paradoxically vindicate Christianity, which would place them in mortal danger within their own world. Some of them were even martyred for their confessions. Thus, we heap insult to injury when we reject their reports in our day.

JOSEPH OF ARIMATHEA AND NICODEMUS

Joseph of Arimathea and Nicodemus were two of the richest men on earth at that time. Joseph of Arimathea was so prominent among the Sanhedrin that he was called "Father" by his peers. He is not mentioned in Matthew, Mark, or Luke because by the time that they wrote their gospels, Joseph of Arimathea had long been exiled from Judea in the Exodus of the Faithful in 36 A.D. with the Mother Mary and apparently had been forgotten as one of the most important characters at the crucifixion of Jesus. John alone mentions him in his gospel because John was an eye witness to the events and saw with his own eyes the tremendous evolvement of Jesus' great uncle.

We only begin to understand Joseph of Arimathea when we begin hearing the echoes of his life from England, where he took the Mother Mary and her associates after the death of Jesus. He later became the "Apostle of Britain" and eventually was canonized with the title of Saint Joseph by the Roman Christians.

With a handful of the respected disciples, Joseph of Arimathea was expelled from Judea by the Sadducees, in a boat without oars or sails -- doomed to drift the oceans wherever God might take them. However, the Sadducees hadn't counted on the fact that Joseph of Arimathea was no stranger to ocean vessels, nor to the sea itself. He had owned fleets of ships that delivered tin and lead around the world from his mines in Gaul (England).

The reader will note that the imprisonment of Joseph of Arimathea as recorded in the writings of Nicodemus was almost as important as the arrest of Jesus Himself. How sad to think that we have forgotten this man who spent his life and fortune defending Jesus before Rome, the Sanhedrin, and the riotous blood-thirsty Sadducees of Jerusalem! What stories could he tell about his Grand Nephew?

A large element of the Pharisees became Christians, like Paul and Nicodemus. Ironically, it may have been the wealth of the Pharisees that sustained the missionary apostles after the death of Christ and facilitated the perpetuation of Christianity throughout the world. Many of the 12 apostles were near paupers, unlike the family and friends of Jesus, and would have needed substantial funds to do what they did after Jesus' death.

THE FAMILY OF JESUS AND THEIR DIVERSIFIED PROPERTY

Among his other distinctions, Joseph of Arimathea was given the title "Noblis Decurio" by the Roman Empire, which meant that he was the chief provider of tin and lead to the entire Roman Empire. Cicero said that it was more difficult to be Noblis Decurio than a Roman Senator! After Joseph, the earthly father of Jesus, had died, Joseph of Arimathea "stepped up to the bar" and provided for the family of Jesus, as was a Jewish custom. Jesus had the opportunity to do many ministerial things from the boats of His own family, but these are still lost to historians.

Joseph of Arimathea's original name was Joseph of Maramore. Marorica was a city in Egypt where Joseph had been born, and was recorded on his burial records when he died in England. One of the reasons that the Holy Family escaped to Egypt in their flight from King Herod after the birth of Jesus, was because the Holy Family had friends, family, and property in Egypt. Most of us would go somewhere familiar if we had to flee, and Egypt offered the Holy Family sanctuary for more reasons than one.

Anna, the mother of the Virgin Mary, was born and raised in Gaul (England) before she pilgrimaged her way back to Bethlehem in her youth and married Joachim, Jesus' grandfather, as she wanted to marry in her faith. Anna and Joseph of Arimathea were brother and sister and had seen much of the known world as children. The title "Heir to the Throne of King David" brought with it lands as well as title. Their family was so wealthy that it provided for a broad cultural foundation for Jesus. We should remember that the heirs to the throne of David were threatened many times when foreign powers conquered Palestine. The heirs to the Throne of David had to "get out of town" to protect their lives. They often remained in exile for centuries, though they maintained their ties with their family and culture and tried to return to marry.

For hundreds of years historians have been looking for information about the mortal life of Jesus in all the wrong places. Many common citizens from India still tell tales of Jesus' historic visits. One may ask the question why is the visit of Jesus to India common knowledge in the streets of the Hindus and yet unknown in the streets of the Christians? How many of those miracles are missing from their rightful place in the Bible?

Jesus personally appears in British legacy, and the Church of England fancies itself the original Christian church for a very good reason. They were practicing Christianity 200 years before the Romans. The first above-ground Christian churches were built in England long before the Romans "got a clue."

History records that the period of 100 years surrounding the birth of Jesus and subsequent the eventual ministry of His apostles, was the most politically stable era that the world had ever known up until that time. This stability had allowed for travel of the common man between countries and had provided for an emerging global economy. It allowed for Jesus to travel during His young life and for the disciples to escape and spread Christianity after His resurrection. It allowed the Mother Mary and her associates to die peacefully in England before Claudius ransacked the island portions of Gaul centuries later.

When Jesus returned to Jerusalem at the end of His travels, He was taxed as a foreigner because he had been out of the country for such a long time with, and for, his wealthy great uncle. This is why many of the common citizens of Judea had lost track of Him after His miraculous birth. His own family in Galilee, like John the Baptist, didn't even recognize Him at their annual feast days just three years prior to His death. Surely they would have recognized Him if He had been there to attend the family reunions every year, a common Jewish custom.

The tax that was levied on Jesus after His return to Galilee was called the "Stranger Tax," not to be confused with one of the temple taxes. Herod often collected these taxes under the direction of Rome. These were taxes designed to collect revenue from merchants of the time, almost like today's sales tax, or import tax. It was strange to see the tax collectors inquiring of Peter why his Master was paying the tax of a foreigner,

> "And when they came to Capernaum, they that collected tribute money, came to Peter and said, 'Does not your master pay tribute?' [referring to the stranger tax] He said, 'Yes.' And when He had come into the house, Jesus spoke first to him saying, 'What do you think Simon? Of whom do the kings of the earth pay custom or tribute, of their own children or strangers?' Peter said unto him, 'Of strangers.' (Matthew 17: 24-25)

Why would Jesus have been paying a stranger tax if He had lived in Galilee all of His young life? How could He have afforded a tax to begin with if He had lived in poverty? Our traditional beliefs about Jesus are obviously incomplete.

Joseph of Arimathea owned palatial mansions in many locations around the world. He had spent a great deal of time with Jesus on his sailing vessels and knew Him as a young man better than anyone else. One can only imagine all the miraculous and inspiring accounts that had transpired between Jesus and His great uncle as they had sailed the world. How many boats had Jesus sailed on? How many storms had He calmed? How many waters had He walked on? We are just now beginning to find some of those stories. Surely Jesus had walked on many parts of the earth and perhaps on many different waters as well.

When Jesus appeared in England, He built an altar and a home for His mother on family owned ground. Maybe he knew that someday His mother would need a place to flee to and to live in after His death, just as their family had done previously. Her tomb is located in England, where she died in 48 AD.

> "It was not, at the time of Jesus, as we shall see, all that uncommon for people from the Middle East to visit England. They had been doing it for thousands of years before the Virgin Mary was born. It is history warped view of the isolation of the British Isles at that time which makes the divine visit to Britain seem so incredible to us. In fact, the traffic was not all one-way. Tradition has it that Anna, Mary's mother, came from Cornwall and had undertaken the journey in the opposite direction." (Did the Virgin Mary Live and Die in England pg. 34)

The family-owned property in England became Holy Ground to the monarchs of the Middle Ages and was used as the most prestigious cemetery for royal families from around Europe. They all wanted to be buried alongside the Virgin Mary, Joseph of Arimathea, Saint Patrick and even King Arthur.

We know that Mary died in 48 AD and that she was 15 or so when she bore the baby Jesus. That would make her late 70's when she died, instead of in her fifties, as the common tradition implies.

WHO WERE THE SCRIBES?

The Scribes were not necessarily a political group within the early church, as were the Sadducees, Pharisees and Essenes. A Scribe therefore, could have also been a member of any Jewish political faction. Cassiodorus said,

> "What happy application. What praiseworthy industry to preach to men by means of the hand, to untie the tongues by means of the fingers, to bring quiet salvation to mortals and to fight the devil insidious wiles with pen and ink. For every word of the Lord written by the Scribes is a wound inflicted on Satan and so, though seated in one spot, the Scribe transverses diverse lands through the dissemination of what he has written."

Not everyone was skilled in those days in the ability to read and write. The Scribes were an instrument of the perpetuation of belief and belonged to each and every faction among the Jews. The authors whose names appear credited in the titles of documents did not personally pen the vast majority of the scriptures. Therefore, the obvious reality is that the writing of scripture was the work, the language, and the literal tongue of the Scribes. They could, and did, change the entire meaning of many texts with the stroke of a pen. Indeed many of the inconsistencies that remain in the Bible and extra-Biblical writings can be attributed to the weakness and the "shorthand" of the Scribes. They were shorthand experts, or to use the technical term "Atachygraphos," which allowed them to take down the "longish" discourses of Jesus and His apostles as they spoke.

The apostle John said, "And there are also many other things which Jesus did, the which, if they should be written everyone, I suppose that even the world itself could not contain the books that should be written." (John 21: 25) Of all the apostles, John should know what he was talking about. He was the best friend of Jesus and had long heard the stories of His life around the campfires. This whimsical impassioned statement by John reflects the extent of the varied life of Jesus that is still not part of the Bible. There were many groups of people who felt the passion after Jesus visited them and recorded His acts in their Holy Writings. The wish of John came true when the tales filled the whole earth from the pens of the local Scribes.

There are two different types of Scribes recorded in history. The worldly scribes were famous in the recording of Greek, Latin, Aramaic and Hebrew. They were well-trained scholars of the day and were responsible for a variety of correspondence and interpretation between languages. These men lived in a multi-lingual society, which required expertise to communicate even within very short geographical distances. Some Jewish Scribes specialized in the scriptural languages and became teachers themselves, experts in religious issues, experts in the written law of Moses and in the oral interpretation of the law that was developed within Rabbinical debate. Some of the disciples of Jesus were considered Scribes, i.e., Mark was schooled in Alexandria for a long time. Paul also is thought to have had "Scribe training."

Jesus himself was literate and at a very young age and taught law to temple priests and wrote many things in His own hand, which we are just beginning to find. (*The Eye Witness of Jesus*) Joseph, Jesus' earthly father had hired a tutor to educate Jesus, but the tutors could teach him nothing. (*Hidden Stories of the Childhood of Jesus*) Jesus was able to communicate directly with Pilate without the need of a translator when He was brought to trial. There are records that portray Jesus and Pilate speaking with each other and using Druid passwords from university debates in England. Both of them had had that experience and they knew that each other had as well. When Jesus was nailed to the cross, the inscription above His head was written in three different languages.

When His followers called Him "Rabbi," they were not referring to His priesthood status as much as referring to His well-known scholastic abilities that had mystified the greatest teachers in Jerusalem and around the world. Had Jesus wished, He could have been the greatest mind the academic world had ever known, or the greatest writer, or the greatest builder, the greatest farmer or the greatest merchant. Instead, He "settled" for being the Savior of the world and to sit with the common people, dressed in common plain clothing of the Nazarene and welcomed the children on His knee. When we really get to know more about Him, and the alternatives He had in His life, Jesus becomes a hero that no tongue can describe.

The problem with many of the translations of scripture, and of Biblical history itself, has originated with the Scribes. For example, the Greek word Tecton in Matthew 13: 55, does not mean carpenter, as is mistranslated in most versions of the Bible; It means builder. We can still recognize the word in our modern term architect. Joseph, the earthly father of Jesus, was not a traditional carpenter, as one might think. He was a great architect, contractor and surveyor, involved in the construction of cities, theaters, and other projects requiring great planning.

When Jesus met Mary Magdalene in the garden after His resurrection, Mary mistakes Him for the gardener, but Jesus addresses her by name. Only then does she turn around and face Him, saying in Aramaic "Rabbuni," meaning, "master." The gardener obviously spoke Aramaic.

It is important to note from the above references the importance and role of the Scribe in Christian history. Without the Scribe, the story of Jesus would never have been told. But with the Scribes, the story of Jesus came out confusing and contradictory.

"It is important to realize that the social arrangement and technology of the first century permitted extremely fast connections between peoples and equally fast development of text. Let us assume, as most scholars would, that this gospel (Matthew) was written somewhere, such as Antioch in the Syrian Province of the Roman Empire. Antakya in southeastern Turkey is situated about three hundred and ten miles north of Jerusalem. Christians, as well as non-Christians, were regular travelers on the road between these two cities. It was, so to speak, a routine journey for private citizens as much as for merchants. A Gospel, or any other book, written in Antioch, and meant to be read in Jerusalem, could have easily have reached its destination within a week. Sent to Rome or Alexandria the parcel would have gone by sea-mail wherever possible. Even allowing for detours, it would have been in the hands of the local community before very long." (The Eyewitnesses of Jesus; pg. 111)

We see another clear example of the language problem necessitating the need for Scribes in the "Render unto Caesar that which is Caesar's" comment of Jesus.

"Between 37 BC and AD 67 not a single coin with a Hebrew or an Aramaic inscription was allowed into, or minted in, Palestine. Text on the coins was Greek. However, in this scene everything depends on the text on the coin right up to Jesus' 'punch line,' which, in any case can not be translated into equally effective Aramaic, 'Give to Caesar what belongs to Caesar and to God what belongs to God.' Indeed such a coin with a portrait of the Emperor Tiberius was anathema to orthodox Jews, while the portrait itself violated the second commandment. The inscription also included the title of Caesar as the son of the Divus Augustus, the god, or deified Augustus.

This was blasphemy, fully understood as such by all those who handled such coins, which made Jesus' conclusion all the more telling...And it was fully understood because it was written in Greek." (The Eye Witnesses of Jesus; pg. 131)

The irony therefore, is that the handlers of the money in the temple had condemned Jesus for His blasphemy, and yet they accepted and used that blasphemy in their own hands. Josephus, the traitorous Jewish historian, used the analogy of Roman coins to punctuate many of the events in his historical Roman apologies.

WHO WERE THE ELDERS AND RULERS OF THE SANHEDRIN?

ELDERS The Greek name for elders is "Presbyteroi." They served as town leaders and assisted in the creation of policies within the community and in the administration of justice. The elders were a "priestly" aristocracy, as the name Presbyteroi implies. They were often the objects of consultation and sat in council over local matters. "The term elders of the city" was not a description of men of age, but rather a description of ecclesiastic position. Joseph of Arimathea was himself an elder and a high priest along with his other titles. Priesthood titles accumulated and were not abandoned as great men advanced in position.

RULERS There was a wide range of princely rulers, local officials, and men of general importance among the people. Nicodemus was one of these men. These rulers were recognized as those to be dealt with in matters of state and religion, because they governed the cities and provinces. They were often very wealthy and were an aristocracy unto themselves. Wealth alone could make a man a ruler in a town. When one of their own emerged with material possessions, it was a matter of pride, something that had alternately been lost and stolen from them for many centuries.

A MACRO-COSMIC LOOK AT THE JEWS AND CHRISTIANS

When the Romans came back to Judea and massacred hundreds of thousands of Jews and Christians, after the death of Jesus, (beginning from the early part of the 30's AD to just after 70 AD), it wasn't because of a military rise of the Jews. Prior to this time, the Jews had not raised their swords against Rome. It was for a reason so shocking that it has been considered as "ridiculous" by modern scholars. The Romans, from their own records, had come back to superstitiously avenge the death of the powerful Jesus that had caused the trembling of the earth, the heavens to darken and the dead to rise in Rome itself. The Romans didn't fully understand the catastrophe in Rome at the death of Jesus, nor did they understand the people that they had blamed, until almost 200 AD, when they themselves began to embrace Christianity. The Romans knew only that these cataclysmic events coincided with the death of the powerful "Healer," on whom Tiberius Caesar had focused his personal interest. The Romans had no other reason to return to Judea and kill the Christians and the Jews.

The Romans were getting rich from the Jews at that time. The lucrative traffic from East to West through Palestine was literally feeding the Empire. When we come to understand how profoundly Jesus had influenced the Caesars, and their family, in Rome, only then we can begin to understand Roman rage against the people who Caesar thought had killed Jesus. The Romans didn't have the custom of ransacking already conquered peoples and seeking their genocide. The Jews were a "money making machine" for the Romans, so the death of the Jews hit them in the wallet, a place they understood well. Rome would never have vowed to exterminate a money making machine without a very good cause. We have lost the Caesar/Jesus connection in history. That road ran straight over Pontius Pilate and his wife Claudia Procula. That road was the eventual reason for both of their deaths.

The early converts to Christianity still considered themselves Jews. In Roman eyes there was no difference. The distinction between Jews and Christians only became clear and permanent after Christianity began to formalize its own structure. Rather than perpetuating the family feeling between the religious beliefs of the world, the emergence of Jesus further polarized, and then separated, the beliefs of the world. Jesus says in the Gospel of Thomas that He did not come to the world to bring peace but rather something very different indeed. In the centuries that followed everyone wanted to own Jesus. The world could not share Him so they fought over Him.

The reason for the combination massacre of Jews and Christians alike in the Roman Coliseums was because the Romans had made no distinction between Christians and Jews. In the eyes of Rome both of them were at fault for the death of Jesus. By the time of Nero, the focus of the martyr turned exclusively to the Christians, but the original reason this group of people was assaulted was ironically because the Caesars thought that Jesus' own people had caused His demise. The word Christian was a "paradoxical blasphemy" in the ears of the Romans who had their own reasons to believe in Jesus. The Romans had heard aloud the shouts of the people in the streets of Jerusalem calling for the death of Jesus and were thus amazed that they eventually called themselves after the title of Christ.

It was easier for the superstitious Romans to believe in the "Healer" Jesus, and the "Man/God" that caused the very earth to quake from a distance at His death, than for the leaders of the Jews to believe in a living Messiah in their own back yard. The very earliest of the Romans, after the death of Jesus, had claimed Him for their own and was the reason that the headquarters of the church eventually wound up in Rome itself. Jesus said it Himself, that a prophet is without honor in his own country. Strangely Jesus was more revered by the hierarchy of Rome than by the leaders in His own land. In the eyes of the Romans, the Jews had killed the "Man/God," and they themselves were the only ones who could avenge Him. Therefore, the Romans avenged Jesus with the blood of His own people.

When the Romans ransacked and preserved the religious artifacts of the temple in Jerusalem in 70 AD, they left for the world a standing pillar giving their reasons for what they did and the list of the artifacts that they hauled off to the Pyrenees. The Roman's didn't melt down the gold and take it to their treasury. They valued the artifacts of the temple. Out of their own mouth, the reason the Romans began the extermination of the Jews and Christians was clearly to avenge the death of Jesus. The reason was literally written in stone for the world to see, even though it sounds strange in our ears today.

Maybe in a bizarre way, the metaphor that Jesus used at His trial, concerning the destruction of the temple, was a "back-handed" prophecy of things to come in more ways than one? Prophecy said that the temple would be destroyed, but Jesus was referring to the temple of His own body. However, like many things that Jesus said, it had multiple meanings. The Romans Destroyed the temple to vindicate Jesus' death. Where is that story of the vindication of Jesus in the destruction of the temple today? Ironically, it wasn't Jesus that brought the temple to ruin but the avarice and hatred of the Sadducees themselves, though the Romans did the deed.

Christianity meant "the followers of The Anointed with oil." Jesus was the fulfillment of the lessor law of Moses. The prophecies of the Messiah clearly outlined the changes to come in the "lessor law." Jesus restored life and power back into a stagnant waiting faith. To a large extent the Christians sit along with the Jews today in that static waiting posture, still claiming to "have it all" while openly rejecting anything new.

Ironically, the Christians themselves refused to continue the succession of spiritual awakening that Jesus had intended. Even the early Christians turned on themselves soon after the death of Christ and plunged the world into darkness for well over a thousand years. The dark days of the condemnation of the Northern Christians for their Southern Christian brothers evolved into the era of inquisition and bloodshed in the name of Jesus. The Bible and historical records are full of the dissention among original local Christian churches. Jesus had prophesied the end of His own literal intent and the resurrection of that movement before He would come again.

Not a single prophet has appeared in the midst of the Jews since Jesus. That should tell them something. Some have feared the emergence of false prophets, and by doing so, opt for none at all. Both the Jews and the Christians continue to fear living prophets of God; neither has any trouble with the dead ones. What will happen when prophets return? Will we still seek their blood? Maybe we should be more afraid that we might kill a real prophet than listen to a false prophet.

Perhaps it would be well to characterize what a false prophet might say and do. A false prophet might claim to be Jesus, but clearly when Jesus returns He will return in all His glory. A false prophet might claim to have the power to perform miracles and then not demonstrate that ability, or only demonstrate that ability for money. A false prophet will clearly have a profit motive, but a real prophet will reject the material wealth of the world as did Jesus and His associates. A real prophet will bring with him discoveries as did Jesus and the ancient prophets. A false prophet will lean on the scriptures and use them to prop him up. There has never been an era of time when the prophets didn't bring with them the reason for their presence. The false prophets will have fatal flaws and have problems with the commandments. The real prophets will be innocent and virtuous figures in their personal lives. If we were to use these simple keys alone, we take away from the false prophets their motivations.

EXTRA-BIBLICAL DOCUMENTS

Truthfully, the extra-Biblical documents were written by human beings and there are human weaknesses and inconsistencies in the texts. However, to call them lies, or outright forgeries, denies a macro-cosmic harmony in the texts, far beyond the ability of any single "apologist" to fabricate. Any well-trained phenomenologist could see the patterns if he weren't too afraid or embarrassed by where those patterns might lead.

In many instances, it has become impolite conversation to discuss a differing religion among one's friends. Mentioning one's religious faith is tantamount to drawing a line in the dirt and defying others to step over it. Jesus spent His life crossing those lines on every possible occasion by sitting and talking with the publicans and the sinners in the public houses of the time, instead of sitting with the learned of His own faith at the walls of the temple, as the pious frequently did. Jesus was scorned by His peers for consistently discussing religion with a wide range of strangers and the "non-anointed." Jesus clearly represented a movement of tolerance, if not total acceptance, among the religious people of the world. Hopefully someday we will all get the "hint" and remember each other as the brothers that we truly are. The place to begin that quest is not to reject one's own traditions outright, but to return to your own house of prayer with the spirit of peace and reconciliation that was the clear message of the Messiah's first visit.

Why would we today be more interested in a mystical character like Nostradomus then in our own ancestral prophets, whose prophetical writings remain outside the Bible, too? The holy prophets have left us with prophecies that dwarf the limited and confusing quatrains of a 16th century mystic medical doctor, who never claimed to be a holy prophet and who used drugs in his spiritual visions. The holy prophets have written prophecy for thousands of years, but have been ignored. Nostradomus will be remembered as the healer of the Black Death and an addict. If we are to believe in prophets, why must we choose one who clearly abused drugs! There are many cultures that misused drugs to induce spiritual experiences. Perhaps we should be more suspicious of these people than those who spoke with clear heads, clean hands, and without a profit motive.

Sequestering and then picking apart individual documents from the holy prophets because of their weaknesses, ignores the main portions of the documents that meaningfully fit into the big picture of mounting Christian evidence. The non-practicing Christian has a greater opportunity than at any other time since the death of Christ, to find and verify Jesus for himself. The rest of the world has a chance to see fulfillment of prophecy unparalleled since the death of Jesus. Ultimately, it will change everything for us all, whether we want it to or not.

It is only natural to be suspicious of spectacular corroboration of your own beliefs with the emergence of modern Christian discoveries, if you haven't heard the evidence before. One of the reasons we do not have more information about Jesus than we do is because writing about Jesus was a sacred task left to the "anointed" and was definitely a capital offense for everyone else. Anyone who thinks that there were hundreds of separate apologists writing about Christianity at the time of Jesus doesn't understand how dangerous such behavior was. If the

Church didn't "string you up," the Romans did. Paradoxically, it was the "anointed" themselves that allowed for oral tradition to creep into and change their scriptures, because it was safer to mingle additional information into existing writings than to have penned a separate work.

Vultures and jackals of our day have singled out and eliminated the weakest and the "diseased" from the herd of ancient writings. They don't appreciate the beauty of the extra-Biblical species. Yet it is the existence of that species that continues to sustain these predators' lives. The jackals would like you to think that they are noble lions that have thinned the herd to purify the scriptural species. Yet, they do their best work in the darkness. We have been in darkness long enough. Let's see what the jackals do in the light of our day of discovery, for a world who wants to know for themselves.

Doesn't corroboration work in both directions? Does it do anyone any good to look for corroboration within the specific extra-Biblical documents and then ignore the corroboration outside the documents contained in extra-Biblical historical literature? Do we need the face of Jesus stamped on a Roman coin before we will believe Jesus had an influence on the Roman Empire during His lifetime? Josephus, the traitorous Jewish historian, would have. He made many of his historical observations based on reference to Roman coins. Josephus was surprisingly a believer of Jesus, but was terrified of Him and largely ignored Him in his writings for good reasons. Josephus wrote his histories at the very tables of those in Rome who were killing the Christians in their coliseums at the time.

We could starve to death for want of the whole scriptural accounts, by being so suspicious. The Jews spiritually starved themselves by ignoring the "Bread of Life" born in their own midst and prophesied by their own holy men. It is time we stop "sweeping the good stuff under the carpet" because of ancient human frailties and powerful hidden agendas.

The phenomena of Jesus pervaded every social fabric and political orientation of His time. The supposed "mythical King of the Jews" caused some very non-mythical disturbances. "Perpetuated myths" is a term that is more descriptive of the colloquial versions of the Jesus, than the real story itself. Will there ever be a time when we can relax and enjoy a good "apology," especially when it is factually based? Why must we fight that which should be easily understood, has broad-based evidence, and is in our own best interest? The "stiff-necked" Jews wouldn't listen. Are we doing any better?

ANNAS, THE KILLER OF JESUS

Annas was the man who had Jesus arrested the night before the crucifixion and paid Judas the 30 pieces of silver for his testimony against Jesus. The guards took Jesus directly to Annas' home after the arrest. Judas threw the ill-gotten 30 pieces of silver back at the feet of Annas in the temple when he realized what he had done to his childhood friend, Jesus. Annas had a bitter secret of his own that had consumed him and his entire family for years. In order to understand Annas we need to acknowledge that the High Priests of the Sanhedrin knew that the Virgin Mary had been chosen to bare the prophesied King of the Jews. There were miraculous events that surrounded her birth and her angelic ministry in the temple that were more than conspicuous to the leaders of the Sanhedrin Council. Nothing could have left the Sadducees with more of a helpless feeling than to have the prophesied mother of the Messiah housed in their own temple and administered to by angels and no way to profit from it.

It was Annas who had "tattled" to the Sanhedrin about Mary's pregnancy to begin with, as if he wanted the story of Mary to be untrue. Joseph and Mary were not yet wed when she was discovered with child by the peering eyes of Annas himself. When Annas gleefully told his fellow priests of the temple that Joseph had secretly married Mary without the blessing of the Church, or even worse had caused her to be pregnant without any marriage at all, a high priest summoned Joseph and Mary to trial in the Sanhedrin court. (see *Hidden stories of the Childhood of Jesus*) Mary and Joseph denied any wrong doing, which meant only one thing to the Sadducean high priests. Mary and Joseph had to pass the deadly test of drinking the poisonous "Waters of the Lord" in order to prove their innocence. Annas knew what trouble "tattling" on Mary and Joseph would cause. He was a high priest who knew about the punishment for violators of Jewish moral laws - especially for those who denied their guilt, as he knew Joseph and Mary would.

When Joseph and Mary returned separately from the mountain, unharmed from the poisonous waters, they were set free. Annas was embarrassed when the Lord spared their lives as a sign that they were telling the truth. Annas spent the rest of his days seeking to destroy Jesus and His family, and ignoring the blatant signs of His divinity, though he himself became the Chief High Priest of the Sanhedrin. His son-in-law and grandson, who became the subsequent

95

Chief Priests of the Sanhedrin, followed in this man's bitter tradition. What would have happened to our history if this one man (Annas) had supported Jesus? Would the first Pope's name have been something like Abraham? Better still, would we all be of one faith?

Annas had hoped that one of the Sadducees of the Sanhedrin, maybe even one of his own family, would have been selected as parent of the expected Messiah, if there was to be a Messiah at all. Abiathar, a friend of Annas, had tried to buy Mary out of the temple for his own son. There is little doubt that each of the ruling Saducean families wanted Mary to be a member of their family.

Mary was one of the most beautiful women of her time. Instead of one of the powerful Saducean families, the parentage honor for the Messiah went to Joseph, a man who was older than Annas himself and a supposed "friend." Joseph was well liked by the Jews, but he had no "political ax to grind." He didn't visibly represent one of the Jewish ruling political factions and therefore could not have added credibility to their politics. Annas felt betrayed by a peer, whom he thought should never have been considered as the spouse of the Virgin Mary in the first place.

Could it have been inspiration that a younger man was not selected as the spouse for Mary? Younger men had the passion of tradition "coursing" through their veins at that time in history. A younger man may not have passed away so soon and allowed the powerful Joseph of Arimathea to take Jesus to the ends of the world in His ministry. The generation of Jesus venerated their family heritages. Standing on your family's name and beliefs was a status symbol in Judea.

Let us return for a moment to the selection process

that paired the Virgin Mary with Joseph. That whole story is in the first book of this series *Hidden Stories of the Childhood of Jesus*. It was Joseph's staff that had sprouted the flower in the temple, in fulfillment of the prophecy of Isaiah, when the Sanhedrin met to decide a spouse for the Virgin Mary. The dove selected the shoulder of Joseph in fulfillment of the voice from the Holy of Holies that was heard by everyone outside the temple and embarrassed the Sadducees among their peers. Joseph, as a possible candidate, hadn't wanted to present his staff to the priests of the temple in the first place. The first round of staffs from eligible bachelors and sons of the Sanhedrin didn't produce the prophesied flower. The voice from the temple told them they had to seek out "he who has not brought his staff to the temple" in a final attempt to fulfill the prophecy of Isaiah. It was the Sadducean candidates who were rejected by Mary and God in favor of a widower who had no aspirations of power to begin with. Joseph was one of the most magnificent and understanding men in the annals of history. It must have appeared that the family of Jesus was destined to offend the Jewish Sadducean leaders on every occasion when Joseph finally emerged as the earthly father of Jesus.

Every time the Sadducees thought they had found a way to turn the people against Jesus, He would perform another miracle and "wow" the public into sympathetic belief. The Sadducees hadn't "strong armed" the issue of Jesus earlier because Jesus was well liked by the people and by many of the wives of the Sanhedrin, as well.

Do not misunderstand. There were those, like Annas, who hated Jesus, just like there are some with hatred in their hearts, who sit on the church benches today. For some, religious belief had become a representation of one's own self image. When a person's self image is in jeopardy they become very defensive - sometimes to the point of anger and hatred. However, one should ask oneself two questions: "Why do we continue to defend tradition at the expense of truth?" and "Why do some feel the need to be the center of attention and be vindicated as individuals?" Annas had risen to the most powerful leadership position among his people, and yet there was one among them that was emerging with more power and influence than he had. It was the green-eyed monster of jealousy that originally corrupted the heart of Annas. Later, Annas felt threatened by the rise of Jesus whom he thought might raise an army and free the Jews from the Romans. Annas couldn't allow his own people to be free from the Romans. That would cost him his position as well.

THE CHRISTIAN "TRIGGER WAS PULLED" AFTER THE DEATH OF JESUS

Many Judeans were just waiting for Jesus to say the word and give them direction as to what they should do. If Jesus had said, "Let's form an army and march on Rome," they would have all risen from their apathy and happily followed Him into battle. Many of the true believers in Jesus were waiting for Him to call for an army to liberate them miraculously from their oppressors. Jesus knew that He had come in the "Meridian of Time" and that about 100 generations would pass before He would return again. Even if they raised an army and won that mythical battle, Jesus knew that the ravages of time would bring that kingdom to

98

its knees many times before the end would come. Political stability would never last as long as the real message of Jesus housed in the hundreds of histories and traditions that dotted the planet.

The Jews were not prepared for the simple sweet message of personal religious awakening. The last three years of Jesus' life, after He had returned from sailing the world, didn't fully give the expectant "Chosen People" the direction they were hoping for. They simply hadn't spent enough time with Him. This lack of strong leadership expected from Jesus made many of the Jewish people as fodder in the hands of the Sadducees who knew exactly what they wanted the public to do with Jesus. The Sadducees used to their benefit, the disappointment of the people and turned their anger towards Jesus for not raising an army to set them free, though they themselves didn't want that job-costing freedom. It was their sarcastic criticism of Jesus that He could destroy the temple and raise it in three days that cost Him his life, rather than some substantial issue not related to military insurrection. The Sadducees had tried to get Jesus to say something directly against the Roman Empire. We see that when Jesus was handed the coin with the face of Caesar on it. Jesus simply replied that they should render unto Caesar what was his and to God that which was His. However, when Jesus metaphorically spoke of the destruction of the temple to the Sadducees, those where "fighting words" that mimicked insurrection.

The recognized leadership from the mouth of Jesus came after His death in the instructions He gave His apostles during the 40 days of His resurrected ministry. After the prophesied resurrection had been fulfilled, the behavior of the apostles took a dramatic change. Most of them had simply fled to their homes and to their former jobs after He was crucified. Apparently, they didn't get the point when Jesus was alive. None of them went home a second time after the 40 days of instruction from Jesus, the Resurrected Being.

It was at this time when the apostles began their real work that the Romans began their extermination of the Jews and Christians. It is amazing that anyone survived, as the Romans slaughtered millions. The small Jewish armies where no challenge at all. There is little wonder why "The Church" became fragmented almost from its inception. There were apostles and other Christians fleeing the Romans, going south, north, east and west - even sailing in ships for very long distances. Was it a coincidence that the message of Jesus was spread so conspicuously throughout the earth after His death? Would His message have ever traveled the earth without the Roman massacres? Would His message have traversed the sands of time had it only stayed in Palestine?

The disbursement of Jesus' message allowed for people around the world to claim at least parts of His message as their own and be among their own protected traditions. The portions of the message that were most important pertained to His message of love and the vanquishing of greed and pride. We see that today disbursed among all the religions of the world. Perhaps this is one good thing that came out of the bigotry and violence of the ancient world. Maybe it didn't matter who preserved His words, only that they were preserved. The unification of His people wasn't as important as individual spiritual growth. Rest assured that there remains a prophetic unification left for the time of our children within the thousand years of peace spoken of as the Millennium era.

If we are ever to understand Jesus, we must stop pointing our fingers at each other and listen to His message that we all partially possess.

THE TRIALS OF CHRIST

TRIAL NUMBER ONE

There were at least four different trials the night of Jesus' arrest. It was a busy night. In John's account, Jesus was arrested at Gethsemane and brought first to the house of Annas, the former Chief Priest of the Sanhedrin. One might wonder why Jesus wasn't taken to some jail, or to the Sanhedrin meeting hall, or to Pilate, Caiaphas (the acting Chief Priest at the time), Herod, or anyone but Annas. The fact that Jesus was taken first to Annas revealed to the world who was personally responsible for Jesus' death. The order of first appearance is very important to the story. Annas' long time vengeance was about to be satisfied.

Jesus stood in the courtyard, or the "Aule," of Annas' house and was questioned by the former Chief Priest. Annas' questions were rhetorical and sarcastic, but Annas was no fool and knew the answer to all his own questions. Annas had seen his own family left out of the movement of Jesus. He had discovered the secret of "Master Mayhem," that a man could kill for gain. An important question for us today is, "How could Annas possibly think that killing Jesus would make it all go away?" The fact that he could even entertain such an idea lets us know how dead the faith was inside this man who had led the Jews.

Jesus was questioned by Annas about His teachings

and was slapped by Annas' attendant when Jesus answered his questions "smartly." Jesus said to Annas that He had not "spoken badly" and asked why the attendant had slapped Him. Peter and John were present among the small crowd in that courtyard. They were there because they had followed along in the crowd, anxious to find out was to happen to the Man they loved. Somehow they mistakenly felt themselves incognito. While warming himself by the fire in the courtyard Peter was asked if he was a companion of Jesus. True to the innocent bystander image he was trying to portray, Peter said he did not know Jesus. This was the first of his three denials.

Annas then sent Jesus to his son-in-law Caiaphas' house to be questioned. It is important that the second person that Jesus appeared before that night was Caiaphas. Obviously the plot to kill Jesus involved the Sanhedrin's Chief Priest of the year. In order to appear with solidarity before Pilate, it required a directive and personal appearance before the Chief Priest, even if the entire Sanhedrin was not present. Caiaphas was the official representative of the Jewish political alliance with Rome.

The crowd mounted as they progressed through the night from place-to-place. As the entourage arrived at Caiaphas' house, Peter was again asked if he was one of Jesus' disciples. Caiaphas knew who Peter was and who was supposed to be present in this group of conspirators. He knew who had been involved in the plot to blackmail Pilate and kill Jesus. Once again, Peter denied Jesus. After the questioning of Jesus by Caiaphas, he sarcastically asked Peter one last time, "Do you know this man?" Peter denied Jesus indignantly, as if he had already answered the question before. Peter was struck in that instant with such guilt that he slithered away into the night and was nowhere to be found by the time Jesus was crucified.

TRIAL NUMBER TWO

Jesus was then lead to his second trial of the evening, in the early morning hours, to the praetorium of Pilate, where Nicodemus records the "bowing of the Standards incident" included in the later text. The account of Nicodemus follows the account of John more closely than it does the accounts of Matthew, Mark, or Luke, because, Nicodemus is physically present at the proceedings with John. The Gospels of Matthew, Mark, and Luke were written long after the events of that night had taken place.

In this meeting Jesus reaffirmed His former statement that He could destroy the temple and rebuild it in three days. By this time apparently a number of the Sanhedrin council, who were friends of Annas and Caiaphas, had gathered before Pilate as the crowd increased in size. Perhaps by their very presence they are implicated in the conspiracy. However, it needs to be understood that the entire Sanhedrin could not have been present. The entire Sanhedrin consisted of 71 men. That would have certainly been a "house full" for the praetorian of Pilate if the whole Sanhedrin, along with the rest of the crowd, had been there. The praetorium simply had room for a dozen men to line the walls with their standard six on each side.

This time a couple of Pharisees expressed their fear that if Jesus was not somehow checked, there would be a Roman reaction that could "Take from us the Jewish holy place" - the temple. The Pharisees had not made their peace with the Romans and were, once again, afraid of any Roman intervention in regards to their possessions. However, we do not hear the Pharisees directly call for the blood of Christ. This comment of the Pharisees was descriptive of their concern for property more than their personal hatred of Jesus, as were the accusations of the Sadducees.

John is the only Gospel where the destruction of the temple is mentioned. This destruction was the predominant theme of the meeting of the Sanhedrin two weeks earlier in a much larger location. The destruction of the temple was the theme the Sadducees had used to incite the Pharisees who had previously acquitted Jesus.

Once again the liberal attitude of the Pharisees was not as blood thirsty as it was with the Sadducees. The Pharisees were concerned over property and Roman intervention. The Sadducees, on the other hand, had been inviting Roman intervention the entire night after Jesus' arrest. The Pharisees had come along through the night in order to moderate the attitudes of their Saducean brothers. This division in attitude is clear. Surely the Pharisees would not have invited Roman intervention in the judgment of Jesus for any reason. The Pharisees hated the Romans, unlike their Saducean counterparts. The Pharisees may not have held the top seat on the Sanhedrin council, but they were more powerful, and had a softer voice, than the Sadducees when they were all gathered together. The Pharisees would not have approached Roman officials to solve their problems on any occasion, for any reason.

TRIAL NUMBER THREE

The trial number three is perhaps the most interesting of the four. Since Pilate found there wasn't a sufficient case to try Jesus, he decided to differ judgment of Jesus to Herod, the head of the Jewish Dynasty. Herod had the power to acquit, or condemn Jesus. Up until this time, there was no love lost between Herod and Pilate. Pilate had disposed Herod as the single monarch in Judea, which had angered Herod. Why then did Pilate send Jesus to Herod? Pilate was not accustomed to defer matters of capital punishment to Herod for any reason, so this action implicated Herod even further in the blackmail scenario. The fact that Pilate sent Jesus to Herod hints at the intrigue between the two former enemies.

Some have thought, because of the circumstances, that Pilate was aloof and simply didn't want to handle matters that were under the jurisdiction of the Jews alone. That could not have been the case at all, because Pilate had been sent to Judea to handle the "King of the Jews" myth.

Pilate also knew that if he condemned Jesus, his wife would be greatly distressed. She had already warned him about her dream the night before. Pilate tried to "pass the buck" back to Herod, but Pilate misunderstood that Herod and the Sadducees didn't just want permission to kill Jesus; they wanted Pilate personally to order Jesus' death. Bouncing Jesus from leader to leader, at the insistence of the Sadducean leaders of the Sanhedrin, appeared like reluctant "ping pong." Neither Herod nor Pilate had ever behaved this way before. Up until this time they had acted like strangers towards each other and had handled matters of state very jealously.

Herod was in Jerusalem for the Passover Feast. He did not live in Jerusalem, but rather in Galilee. Strangely Herod neither acquitted Jesus nor condemned Him, even though he had condemned to death every one of his potential threats in his past. He had even killed his wife and children and brothers. Why didn't he simply order Jesus' death? Herod knew he had the blackmail on Pilate and sent Jesus back to him, which was the original plan to begin with.

We know the attitude of Herod because of what he said when Jesus was brought before him. Herod obviously had no intentions of personally condemning Jesus to death and was confident that Jesus should be killed by the order of Pilate. Herod began his inquisition of Jesus by trying to satisfy his own long-held curiosity. But he was more interested in the potential "magic" of Jesus than in His guilt. When Herod saw Jesus,

> "he rejoiced greatly, for much time he had been wishing to see Him because of what he had heard about Him. Indeed he was hoping to see some signs done by Him. Jesus said, 'You will not see what is granted to those of faith. Many kings have wished to see what you see and have not seen, and to hear what you hear and have not heard.'"

The traveling Jesus had been tempted by Kings of other lands before to perform miracles in front of their eyes. Herod then gave Jesus a purple robe of royal mockery and sent Him back to Pilate. Rest assured that Herod never gave a royal purple robe of authority to anyone who might have threatened his throne, even in jest. He surely wouldn't have released Him for any reason if he had been given permission by the Roman Governor to kill Him. Jesus had been a threat to Herod's father and had been a threat to Herod himself all his life. Obviously there was something going on between Herod and Pilate that is not part of the Biblical story. That secret was blackmail.

The Sadducees had already delegated Pilate as the "Patsy," and Herod "laughed off" the visit of Jesus and sent Him back to Pilate. Herod needed the death of Jesus to be the fault of Pilate.

TRIAL NUMBER FOUR

In this trial Jesus is brought back to Pilate, who had only two options left. He tried to "sing and dance" his way out of killing Jesus; however, there was still the stench of blackmail in the air.

Pilate tried to use the Jewish custom of releasing a prisoner on the day of Passover to justify releasing Jesus. However, Passover was a Jewish holiday, not a Roman one, and therefore of no concern to Romans. Herod himself, not Pilate, administered the jails, and it was Herod who was customarily in charge of releasing one prisoner on the day of Passover. Barabbas, a known murderer and strongly disliked by the Jews, was released in the stead of Jesus. There are many that have thought the real name of Barabbas was Jesus as well, and thus the confusion over whom should be killed. Whether the real name of Barabbas was Jesus or not, everyone knew who would be the real victim.

The desperate Pilate tried one last time to free Jesus

by using what he thought was favorable public opinion toward Jesus. Pilate knew from his wife how many of the Jews had followed and venerated Jesus. So Pilate stood before the crowd and asked why they wanted this man to die? Pilate thought that he was voicing a rhetorical question to the Jews who had thrown palms beneath Christ's donkey upon entering the city of Jerusalem and surely must want to free Him.

However, the Chief Priests and Scribes had gone about the city with a publicity campaign against Jesus. They had told the people that this bound and chained Jesus would never liberate them from their bondage. They were enormously successful because the very people who had previously shouted praises for Jesus now were shouting for His blood only a few hours later. Nothing could speak lower of these people than their remarkable change of heart. Why else did the crowd change from sympathy for Jesus to "lynching" status? When the Chief Priests Annas, Caiaphas, and their attendant "minions," saw Jesus, they yelled, "Crucify Him! Crucify Him!" And the people followed the lead of their rulers. Pilate said to them, "Take Him yourself and crucify Him. For I do not find a case against Him." The high priests answered Him, "We have a law, and according to the law, He ought to die because He has made Himself God's son."

> "When Pilate heard this statement he was even more afraid and he went back into the preatorium and said to Jesus, 'From where are you?' and Jesus did not give him an answer. So Pilate said, 'Do you not speak to me? Do you not know that I have the power to release

you and the power to crucify you?' Jesus answered, 'You have no power over me at all except what was given to you from above. Therefore, the one who gave me over to you has the greater sin.'"

"Now Pilate having heard these words led Jesus outside and set Him on the Judgement seat. Now it was Preparation Day for Passover. It was the sixth hour." (noon, the traditional and prophetic time of the killing of the sacrificial lambs in the temple) "Pilate said to the Jews, 'Look your king.' They yelled out, 'Take Him and crucify Him.' Pilate said to them, 'Shall I crucify your King?' The Chief Priest answered, 'We have no king but Caesar.'"

This is obviously rhetoric of the Sadducees and not of the Pharisees. The Pharisees hated the rule of the Romans, the Sadducees were the only Roman allies among the Jews. "Then he gave Jesus over to them in order that He be crucified." In the end the Sadducees had to personally handle the actual crucifixion anyway. Why would Pilate encourage the people of Jerusalem to view Jesus as a king in the first place? Pilate was obviously more desperate than history gives him credit.

The only common memory of the Roman treatment of Jesus is the bestial lashing given Jesus by the Roman guard on the day of His death. The lashing was the traditional "Third Degree" punishment given by the Romans to condemned men. This same "Third Degree" lashing was used by the Christian leaders of the inquisitions over a thousand years later. Pilate was forced to follow

Roman tradition or be betrayed before Tiberius. However, at Pilate's direction, his personal servants placed their handkerchiefs and robes on the floor where the wounded Jesus was to walk in order to cushion His path. Pilate didn't request that other condemned men have linen placed under their feet as they walked to their death. He wouldn't have tolerated that at all.

History records that one of these kerchiefs was eventually sent to Tiberius and became his personal artifact from Jesus' crucifixion. We must ask ourselves why would Tiberius want a kerchief from the feet of Jesus as his personal artifact?

Tradition records that Tiberius was ultimately healed of his affliction by a picture created by Jesus and preserved by Veronica, one of Jesus' faithful disciples. (That story is included in the text below.) If you heal Caesar of his afflictions, you have more than his interest. If you kill Caesar's potential "healer," you incur his wrath. It was that simple. Caesar may not have understood Christianity, but he did understand the power of Jesus. It may have paradoxically been this very need for a healing that sparked the vengeful anger in the heart of Caesar when Jesus was crucified and caused Caesar to unsheathe the swords of his legions against the Jews.

The superstitious Tiberius thought that he alone could have protected Jesus from Jesus' own people. When Pilate permitted the crucifixion of Jesus, Tiberius angrily had his head served to his wife on a platter, but not before Pilate made his peace with his personal Savior. History records that Procula, Pilate's wife, also died at that moment, not totally of grief, but of a magnificent overwhelming spiritual acquiescence.

JUDAS

The Sadducees originally thought that Judas would be a valid and powerful witness against Jesus on the charge of blasphemy. He had told the Sadducees, in sworn testimony before the Sanhedrin, that Jesus had referred to Himself as "The Son of God." After all, Judas was one of the special twelve and well known to have been a childhood friend of Jesus. This witness would have been useful to the Sadducees, but was of no use to the Romans. The Romans were not interested in the charge of blasphemy because they didn't care about defaming a Jewish god. This is why the guard that arrested Jesus couldn't have been a Roman guard, but rather was the Sanhedrin Police Force. Judas never appeared in the trials after his fateful kiss.

If Pilate had wanted to identify Christ, he had 100 political allies who would have recognized Jesus anywhere, including his own wife, without the kiss of Judas. If the Sadducees wanted to identify Jesus, any one of them could have done the job. It was the Sanhedrin Police Force, under the directions of Annas and then Caiaphas, that had used Judas to seal his testimony against Jesus with a kiss. Ironically that kiss condemned Judas more than it did Jesus and was utterly wasted.

Judas was going to spent the 30 pieces of silver he received for betraying Jesus on an acre of ground that has come to be known as the "acre of blood" or the "Hakeldamach" in Hebrew. The silver coins came from the temple treasury, and Judas attempted to give the money back, in his subsequent guilt, by throwing the coins at his benefactor's feet in the temple; but they refused to touch it as it spilled upon the floor.

Matthew, Mark, and Luke weren't present at the various trials of Jesus, and each told a very different story of how Judas died. He was recorded to have contracted a loathsome disease, or been crushed by a wagon that burst him open or hung by his own hand (book of Matthew). At the Last Supper Jesus had said, "Woe to that man for whom it would have been better not to have been born." Josephus reports Ahithophel saying, "It was better for him to withdraw from life freely and high mindedly by choosing hanging than by being punished later." (Ant. 7.9.8; number 228-29) We must ask why Josephus would care more about the story of Judas than the story of Jesus? Obviously Josephus knew more than he was telling when he wrote his histories at the table of the Caesars.

WHERE WERE THE APOSTLES?

Nine of the apostles had fled town when the Jewish police at Gethsemane brought Jesus to trial after his arrest. These were men who were not yet trained well enough by Jesus to fulfill a great mission. They didn't even stand by Him during his darkest hour in the garden and left the scene when He was arrested. Judas was no longer in the fold of the twelve apostles. Only Peter and John, accompanied by Nicodemus and Joseph of Arimathea, went to the trial before Annas.

At the crucifixion, "John the Beloved" was the only apostle present to witness the bloody ordeal, along with Mary (Jesus' mother), Mary (the wife of Cleophas and a

113

sister-in-law to Mary), Solome (the midwife at the birth of Jesus), Mary Magdalene, Mary and Martha, (the Bethany sisters). Peter had slithered away in shame for what he had done. Ultimately, the women in the life of Jesus stood by Him to the end.

As Joseph of Arimathea and Nicodemus carried the lifeless body of Jesus to Joseph's own tomb, the very earth came apart at the seams. Apparently, Joseph and Nicodemus didn't have time to completely prepare the decimated body of Jesus during that terrible destruction. They just wrapped Him in linen and hurriedly poured a hundred pounds of mixed spices over the body and rolled a huge stone in front of the tomb to protect it until things could settle down a little.

By time the Sabbath had arrived, the earth had quieted. Joseph of Arimathea was back in Arimathea, after the spirit of Jesus had removed him from the locked room with no windows and told him to stay in Arimathea until called upon. Mary Magdalene, the Mother Mary, and Solome had come to the tomb to properly prepare the body of Jesus. They surely would have brought Joseph of Arimathea had they not thought he was still imprisoned. Mary Magdalene found the linen and spices used by Nicodemus and Joseph of Arimathea on the floor. Many have wondered if the preparation of the body was a two-step process. The reality was that there was insufficient time to do the job properly the first time. The women waited three days because of the terrible destructions that were taking place. When they arrived, they found the stone rolled away. The guards, under the direction of Joseph, were not visibly present, but were hiding close by and observed everything.

These sweet women, who loved Jesus, had come to

Jesus' tomb by themselves. They were carrying with them a basket of cooked eggs for the guards at the tomb, almost like a peace offering that would allow them to prepare the body. This basket of cooked eggs remains as part of our Easter tradition. When they saw that the stone had been rolled away they feared that either the storms had rolled it away or that the enemies of Jesus had moved it and absconded with the body and thrown it into a pit.

A young man, whom they did not recognize at first, was sitting on the ledge inside the tomb and obviously very much alive. It must have been an angel, maybe Jesus Himself, and he told the women to go and tell the apostles that Jesus had risen from the dead and was in Galilee waiting for them. The apostles by this time had returned to their traditional homes and jobs because they figured that everything had come to an end. The terrible destructions must have also disoriented the apostles and their disciples, as well.

The women quickly ran to tell the apostles. There were probably a lot of people in shock around town at the time. The earthquakes and storms had brought the city and many of its buildings to ruin. There were even appearances of people who had risen from the dead walking around town and lamenting the wickedness of the Jews. Why was this story left out of the Bible?

It is important to note that the resurrected Jesus didn't run and hide from anyone, nor did He disappear in the midst of the day. He walked openly in the streets of Jerusalem and appeared in route to Galilee and later walked with His apostles and disciples and was seen by all. When Jesus began His 40-day ministry after his crucifixion, Pilate and at least 500 other recorded witnesses saw Him in His resurrected form. There were in actuality many more than that. The fact that so many people saw Jesus walking the streets after His crucifixion has given rise to the myth that Jesus was not dead when He was taken from the cross. However, if He had been taken down alive from the cross He certainly wouldn't have been in any condition to walk the streets either.

AFTERMATH

JOSEPH OF ARIMATHEA'S ARREST

Joseph of Arimathea had his own experience in being arrested by the Jews. After Joseph had petitioned for the body of Jesus from Pilate, and had transferred it to his own tomb, he had one of the most incredible spiritual experiences in all Christendom.

With Nicodemus, Joseph had been accosted by the Sanhedrin Police Force inside the only synagogue left standing after three days of destruction. Caiaphas and Annas were angry with Joseph because he had "snatched" the body of Jesus "out from under their noses," and by doing so, had encouraged potential rumors of Jesus' resurrection from the dead. The Sadducean leaders of the Sanhedrin arrested Joseph of Arimathea and intended to keep him locked up for three days until after the prophesied resurrection was to have occurred. The Sadducees didn't want Joseph to be free to play a resurrection game on them. While Joseph was locked in a room with no windows, a guard outside the door, and only one key possessed by Caiaphas himself, Joseph had a vision of Jesus' travels in the world of the dead. Joseph was physically whisked away from his sealed prison by the crucified Jesus and returned to his own home in Arimathea, where he was told by Jesus to remain until called upon.

When Jesus was resurrected on the third day, there

117

were many others resurrected with Him, namely Moses, Abraham, Isaac, Jacob, Adam, Noah and countless others. There were rumors of resurrections in Rome itself. There are historical records that cite the rising of the dead also in foreign lands far distant from Judea. One can only imagine the shock on the part of a superstitious Caesar in Rome when among the destructions of his city were dead men rising. Ancient prophets were seen in the streets of Jerusalem lamenting the terrible mistake that had been made by their descendants, the Jews. Many recorded the wales in the streets and heard the resurrected cries of the risen. Perhaps another reason that Caesar returned to Palestine to exterminate the Jews and Christians was because of the language of the walking dead in Rome who knew of Jesus.

Pilate himself saw and heard things that caused him to surround himself with 50 armed guards and to go look for this risen Jesus. His wife had already seen Jesus walking about and had told her husband. If there was one event that wins the award for the greatest surprise in history, it must have been the meeting of Pilate with the resurrected Jesus, whom he just caused to be crucified. That adds a brand new meaning to the word "whoops."

HEROD THE KING, OR HEROD THE GREAT: THE EARLY HEROD

Many different Herods affected the life of Jesus. Herod the King was the first Jewish "Client King" of the Romans in the Eastern Province. "Herod" was a title, like the term "Caesar" was a title. Herod "Antipas" the King was the same Herod that issued the extermination order to kill all the babies, two years and younger, after the birth of Jesus. He was the same king that mistakenly ordered John the Baptist's father, Zacharias, to be murdered between the altar and the front door of the temple while looking for the Baby Jesus. Herod thought that John the Baptist was the prophesied Baby King of Israel.

He reigned from 37 to 4 BC, levying heavy taxes on the Jews, conscripting labor, and building massive public works projects. He was the one who built the first underwater concrete port for the merchant vessels. This seaport was the goose that laid the golden egg for Herod, and the Jews and Romans as well, and allowed the East and West to be connected as never before.

THE CONFUSING TITLE OF HEROD

After the death of Herod the King, his territory was divided among three of his sons, Archelaus, Philip and Antipas. Archelaus was the Herod in Jerusalem that the angel described to Joseph (the earthly father of Jesus) while he was in Egypt. The angel said to Joseph that the Herod that had sought the baby's life was dead and Archelaus sits on his throne. It was now safe for Joseph and his family to return to home. The immediate threat for the Baby Jesus was derailed by the infighting between the three sons of Herod the King. However, the Herod who emerges during Jesus' adult ministry, as Tetrarch in Galilee, is Antipas the second, who governed from 4 BC to 39 AD. Herod Antipas the Tetrarch had exiled one brother and had dealt with the other by the time Jesus returned from the sea to perform the last three years of His ministry among His own people.

Galilee was the center of commerce at that time, while Jerusalem was the hub of religion and the location of the temple. There were Biblical, and non-Biblical references that coined the phrase that "Nothing good ever came out of Nazareth." That phrase came long afterward because there wasn't a city called Nazareth during the infancy of Jesus. That statement originated because Nazareth was a center of foreign commercial traffic and experienced the street life associated with that type of commerce. However, Galilee was the home of the majority of Jesus' disciples and contained His largest following.

Jerusalem was a dangerous place for Jesus, as he was a rich kid from the "wrong side of the tracks." One needs to remember that Jerusalem was the ancestral home of the tribes of Judah and Benjamin. Galilee, to the north, was the ancestral home of the other ten tribes. There had been civil war for between these two sections of the country for 300 years prior to the birth of Jesus caused by the treatment of one of the princesses of Benjamin. There was fierce competition and prejudice among the tribal Hebrew nation. Jesus, as a leader of the Jews, was from the wrong town, much like having a non-Italian Pope in our day. Jesus would never have been crucified in Galilee where thousands of people hung on His every word. It appears that even Herod was powerless against Jesus when He was in Galilee. Jesus couldn't have been crucified in the land south of Jerusalem either, for had He been walking the streets of Edom, the Essenes would have risen up in Jesus' defense. After all, Jesus had performed a great ministry among the Essenes, the communal societies of the south, and He wore the simple dress of the Essene population. It was Jerusalem that was the "Achilles Heel" for Jesus.

HEROD OF JESUS' TIME

Herod Antipas the Tetrarch beheaded John the Baptist and worried that Jesus was John the Baptist come to life again. The real shocker for most Christians, who know the story of John the Baptist, is that Jesus Himself baptized more people than John the Baptist ever did. It was this baptism behavior of Jesus that caused the confusion in the mind of Herod, thinking that John the Baptist had returned from the dead. His father had tried to kill John the Baptist at the time of the birth of Jesus and had killed Zacharias in the process. Apparently King Herod had told his son Herod Antipas the Tetrarch that the King of the Jews was the son of Zacharias, the High Priest of the temple. Therefore, Herod was more afraid of a resurrected John the Baptist than he was of Jesus in the flesh.

Herod obviously knew of the resurrection rumors prior to the death of Jesus, or He wouldn't have thought Jesus to be a resurrected being during his lifetime. There had never been a resurrection prior to Jesus. Since resurrection was a concept housed within the written Messiah Prophesies that could not be accessed within Jewish synagogues. That teaching was only contained within oral traditions in Palestine. The confusion between John the Baptist and Jesus could have existed only because Jesus had not physically been present in Palestine during most of His life, and John the Baptist had spent many years in the desert. Had either one of these two men been seen with thousands of disciples walking the public streets prior to the final ministry of Jesus, there wouldn't have been confusion in the minds of anyone.

Luke is the only one to mention Herods (plural). In Luke, Christ rebuked Herod in absentia as "The Fox." It was this Herod the Tetrarch that appeared before Pilate when Pilate told the Sanhedrin that he didn't want to be personally involved with the death of Jesus.

This Herod and Pilate had begun their relationship as competitive enemies. Herod was not accustomed to leadership competition. His father had made a political alliance with Rome that left him in sole power as the heir to the deposed throne of David. In the mind of Herod, Pilate interfered in that original treaty. Both Pilate and Herod thought separately that they should administer the affairs of the province. In fact, each of them had separate and independent powers over the province. Pilate acted as an overseer, while Herod ran the daily civil affairs of the country i.e., the administration of jails and local police. One of the major hidden agendas for Pilate was to watch for the Messiah King who could inspire insurrection. However, the "Jesus ordeal" brought Herod and Pilate together as "strange deathbed fellows" who began to correspond with each other at the end of their lives and who shared their feelings over the death of Jesus. (See one of those letters later in this text.)

Herod Agrippa, the son of another brother of Herod Antipas the Tetrarch, named Aristobulus, the grandson of Herod the Great, as the next ruler in Galilee until 44 AD. This is the Herod that executed James, the son of Zebedee, the second cousin of Jesus, and imprisoned Peter in Acts 12, only to be subsequently struck down by an angel and eaten by worms. The Herod dynasty had a miserable way of dying.

Josephus said, "Agrippa the King, was clothed in a

robe woven with silver, and was a spectacle in the theater of Caesarea. When the people saw that his raiment flashed, they said to him, 'Before we feared you as a man; now we believe you are exalted above the nature of mortals.' Herod saw an angel standing over him and he smote him to death." Once again it is amazing that Josephus recounted the heavenly punishments of Herod and yet mentioned Jesus so little in his histories. Josephus definitely knew the story of Jesus well enough to tell, but apparently didn't because of the Caesars.

Herod Agrippa number two, son of Agrippa number one, was the ruler who listened to Paul during his Caesarean imprisonment between AD 57-59.

Let's return for a moment to the Herod of Jesus' time. Herodias, the wife of Herod Antipas the Tetrarch, desired the death of John the Baptist. She had been married to Herod Philip, but deserted him for his half-brother Herod the Tetrarch, who was in power by that time. She had "slept her way up the ladder" of power. The peripheral Herod family was considered royalty, like the Magi Kings that had come from the "East" at the birth of Jesus. The conflict between John the Baptist and Herodias began when John started preaching about her need for repentance and the imminent coming of the Christ (anointed with oil). Herod was upset over John's reference to his sinful relationship with Herodias. Luke says, he added to his sins by locking John up in prison.

The real sin of Herod was that Herodias was Herod's own niece. He had divorced his wife for an incestual romance. One day Herodias' daughter Solome, Herod's grand niece, and stepdaughter at the same time, danced for Herod and his guests. Herod had already proved that he liked to keep romance in the family. It was Solome who required the head of John the Baptist as a lusty favor for her performance. "Mama" Herodias shamefully had a hand in that whole thing as well.

Herodias had her final judgement for what she had done and was banished to Gaul with Herod "Philip," her former husband, after the Roman Emperor made Herod Agrippa Tetrarch. Herod Antipas the King had already died of a terrible disease. Herod Antipas the second is the one who writes the first letter in the following text beginning with the death of his young daughter coincidentally named Herodias as well. Herodias paid a dear price for the beheading of John the Baptist, but banishment must have seemed pleasant in comparison with the other things that had happened to her in life.

THERE WAS ONE LAST GRUESOME SERIES OF DEATHS

When the earth came apart at the seams after the death of Jesus, there were many members of the Sanhedrin that died in that event. There are reports that the earth simply opened up and swallowed them up, as happened to some of the rebellious Israelites that built the golden calf in front of Mount Sinai while Moses was on the mountain receiving the Ten Commandments. Ironically, some of the very members of the Sanhedrin that had condemned Jesus, spent their last few hours on earth angry with the very Messiah that was in the process of resurrecting their dead prophets. Caiaphas survived the ordeal, along with Annas. However, Annas died a short time later when the Romans began their purge. The dead body of Annas was thrown into the streets as "food for the dogs." It was Caiaphas's son, Anninias, who became the next high priest of the Sanhedrin and witnessed the bloodshed from the Romans who came to avenge the death of Jesus caused by his father.

The slaughter of the Christians and the Jews that followed was one of the bloodiest episodes in the history of the world. The blood shed over the death of Christ hasn't stopped today. This one event has cost more lives than any plague in the history of the world, including the flood of Noah. Surely the heavens see death differently from mortal men. For some, death is a testament to their honor. For others, it is merely the end of their evil. In either case, death has punctuated the story of Christ for many millions.

For those, who see death as the end of existence, they cannot understand a bloodthirsty God who would allow the slaughter of His "chosen" people. For others, who believe in the continuation of life after death, the only meaning of an inevitable death is the way we have lived our lives. Surely Jesus had more to say about the way men should live than any single person did in history. Death has been a paradoxically merciful end to many that had allowed their lives to begin a geometrical descent into wickedness.

Caiaphas, the wicked Chief Priest of the Sanhedrin, died in 36-37 AD at the hands of his allies, the Romans. The bones of Caiaphas were discovered in 1990 south of the walled portion of Jerusalem and not in a traditional cemetery. The Romans paradoxically avenged Jesus after all.

APOLOGY? -- -- I'M DOWN RIGHT SORRY!

On the surface some of the things said by Ananias, the Roman Centurion who gathered the writings of Nicodemus, sound like they are dripping with sweet Christian syrup. However, ponder for a moment. The climate of that era was not only hostile against Christian heresies, but was also mortally dangerous from the hands of the Romans. It was not a healthy behavior to be writing about the miraculous events that tied Romans and Jews together.

Josephus says that Justin, the historian responsible for the later preservation of this research by Ananias, was his own contemporary. Therefore, the "Writings of Nicodemus" are even more authentic.

Ananias was a man who felt the sorrow and burden of an ancient people on his shoulders. No one had said they were sorry for the death of Jesus. In his mind no one had felt the blame. Here is a man who spent a great deal of time bringing together an inspirational vignette in history and was deeply moved by the injustice of the villains and the grandeur of the heroes.

In the end he asks, "Therefore, all you who read this, and copy it out, remember me and pray for me that God may be gracious to me and forgive my sins which I have sinned against Him. Peace be to those who read and hear it, and to their servants. Amen!" He was all by himself and telling a story for a rhetorical audience that could never really respond to him.

How would you have said you were sorry if you were Roman and had seen that your own people played a part in the death of the very Messiah you have come to know? This was not an issue of one man's death. It was an issue of the conflict between the heavens and the earth. Ananias was a man who felt caught alone between the heavens and the earth, writing a sacred history for himself. The Christians rejected his writings because he was Roman and not of Christian blood. How many histories have been rejected because "accepted" families didn't write them? There are thousands of histories of Jesus that we hide from ourselves today for that very reason. There wasn't yet an audience among the Romans. When the Romans did choose to get on the "Christian wagon," they too, rejected their own histories, though they preserved them in their libraries for our day. Those who think that Ananias was a foe of Christianity badly missed his message and the climate in which he wrote. Maybe instead of a "tongue in cheek" acceptance, we need to look inside this one for the very flavor of the heavens themselves. Christians, like the Jews, shunned their own history with the bigotry of the word "heresy." Who really perpetuated the real heresy? How many times have the flock rejected the lost sheep who Jesus said were more valuable than the ninety and nine?

Have you ever said something so heart-felt that it sounded a little too sweet for callused ears? A "lying apologist" would surely have written a "tamer" story than this. A "lying apologist" wouldn't have included as many facts in his myths that could have either been corroborated or exposed as lies. Just because parts of Nicodemus sound a little "sappy" doesn't mean that they weren't sincere, or that the events weren't real.

IMPORTANT POLITICAL LETTERS

OVERVIEW OF THE LETTERS BETWEEN PILATE AND HEROD

The only requirement for understanding the letters of Pilate and Herod is a basic knowledge of the story of the crucifixion of Jesus, which we have just discussed.

These letters, written in a Syriac manuscript, exist in a British museum. This particular version is from the sixth century, which in turn was copied from the originals. They also appear in Paris written in Greek. We must understand that the original manuscripts had a shelf life of only a couple of hundred years. We must also understand that at the fall of the Roman Empire in the fifth century many of the secret documents came out of hiding. This translation has been rewritten to make it more readable. The fact that the letters are corroborated from two different sources makes them most credible.

LETTER OF HEROD TO PILATE, THE GOVERNOR

I am experiencing great anxiety. I am writing to you so that you might feel my pain with me. My daughter Herodias, who is dear to me, was playing upon a lake covered with ice. The ice broke under her, and as she passed through

128

the ice, the ice cut off her head. Her head remained on the surface of the ice on the lake. Her mother is now crying and holding the head of her daughter in her lap. My whole house is in great mourning.

I heard that you wished to see me because you have seen Jesus again after His resurrection. I know that you wanted me to see, and hear Him also, as one man speaks to another. It is certain that because of the many evil things, which I had done to John the Baptist, and because I mocked the Christ, I received my own reward at the death of my daughter for the blood of other people's children, which I have shed upon the earth. The judgments of God are righteous; for every man receives according to his thought. However, I thought that since you were worthy to see that God-Man after his resurrection, I would ask you to pray for me.

My son Azbonius is also in the agony of death. I too, am in great pain because I have the dropsy. I am in great distress because I persecuted John who introduced baptism by water. Therefore, my brother, the judgments of God are correct. My wife, through grieving for her daughter, is become blind in her left eye, because she desired to blind the eye of righteousness.

The Lord said, "There is no peace for the doers of evil." There has already come great affliction upon the priests, and upon the writers of the law, because they delivered unto you the ruler of the world. Through their deeds they have consented that the Gentiles should become heirs of the kingdom. For the children of light shall be cast out for they have not observed the things, which were preached concerning the Lord, and concerning His Son.

Take courage with your wife when you remember that

the kingdom belongs to the gentiles. For we, the chosen people, have mocked the Righteous One.

We would like to be buried by you, rather than being buried by the priests who will experience the vengeance from the death of Jesus Christ. Good luck to you and your wife Procula. I am sending you the earrings of my daughter and my own ring as a memorial of me and my family. Already there are worms from my body as a judgment for the things which I have done. I am afraid of that judgment to come after my death. Both of us will stand before the living God and receive an eternal judgment.

LETTER OF PILATE TO HEROD.

Pilate to Herod the Tetrarch: Peace

When you delivered Jesus to me, I took pity on myself and testified by washing my hands that I was innocent concerning Him who rose from the grave after three days. You desired me to be associated with you in His crucifixion. But I learned from the executioners, and from the soldiers who watched His sepulcher, that He rose from the dead. I have especially confirmed what was told me, that He appeared bodily in Galilee, in the same form and
with the same voice, and with the same doctrine, and with the same disciples. He was preaching with boldness about His own resurrection and an everlasting kingdom. Behold, the heaven and earth rejoice. Procula my wife believes in the vision which appeared unto her which spoke of what would happen to me when you sent me Jesus to be delivered to the Jews.

130

Now when my wife Procula heard that Jesus was risen and had appeared in Galilee, she took Longinus the centurion and twelve soldiers with her to find Jesus. They were the same that had watched at the sepulcher. They went to see this great spectacle and found Him with His disciples. While they were standing, and wondering, and gazing at Him, Jesus looked at them and said to them, "What do you want? Do you believe in me now Procula? Remember the covenant, which God gave to the fathers. It is said that every body who had perished should live by means of my death, which you have now seen. Now, you see that I live, the man who your husband had crucified. I suffered many things, till I was laid in the sepulcher. But now, hear me and believe in my Father -- God, who is in me. For I loosed the cords of death and I shall come again."

When my wife Procula and my guard had heard these things, they came and told me, weeping. I suffered because of what they had told me. I arose and put on a garment of mourning and took with me my wife and fifty Romans and went into Galilee. When I was in route to see this Jesus for myself, I testified that you, Herod, did these things through me. It was you who counseled with me and constrained me to arm my hands against Him, and to judge Him that judgeth all, and to scourge the Just One. When we drew nigh to Him, a great voice was heard from heaven, and a dreadful thunder, and the earth trembled, and gave forth a sweet smell, like unto that which was never perceived, even in the temple of Jerusalem.

Now while I stood in the way, Jesus saw me as He stood and talked with His disciples. But I prayed in my heart, for I knew that it was He whom you delivered to me. I knew He was Lord of created things and Creator of all. When we saw Him, all of us fell upon our faces before His feet and I said with a loud voice, "I have sinned, O Lord, in that I sat in judgement over you, you who are the avenger of truth. I know that you are God, the Son of God. I only saw you as human and not as divine. Herod, with the priests of the Sanhedrin, constrained me to do evil against you. Have pity, therefore, upon men, O God of Israel!"

My wife, in great anguish, said, "God of heaven and of earth, God of Israel, reward me not according to the deeds of Pontius Pilate, nor according to the will of the Sanhedrin priests, nor according to the thought of the sons of the priests; but remember my husband in your glory!"

Now our Lord drew near and raised my wife and I and the Romans up, and I looked at Him and saw the scars from the cross upon him. And he said, "I am He who the prophets had foretold would come, and He who was not recognized by them when I did come. I am the Son of Man, the Son of the Most High, who is forever. I arose from the dead, and am glorified on high by all that He created, and established for ever and ever."

End of the Letter of Pilate to Herod.

THE REPORT OF PILATE, THE GOVERNOR

The next two letters are mirror images of each other, for the most part, but do contain slight differences, so they are both included here. Apparently Pilate wanted to say substantially the same thing to both Tiberius Caesar and one of the Augustus Caesars in Rome.

Concerning our Lord Jesus Christ, which was sent to Augustus Caesar, in Rome.

To the most potent August, divine and awful Augustus Caesar, Pilate, the administrator of the Eastern Province:

I have received information, most excellent one, and as a result I am seized with fear and trembling. For in this province which I administer, is a city called Jerusalem. In that city the whole multitude of Jews delivered unto me a certain man called Jesus and brought many accusations against Him, which they were unable to establish by consistent evidence. They charged Him with one Jewish heresy in particular; namely, that Jesus said the Sabbath was not a day of rest. He had performed many cures on that day. He made the blind see, the lame walk, raised the dead, cleansed lepers, healed the paralytic and gave them power to walk and run, removing their infirmity by His word alone.

There is another very mighty deed, which is strange to the gods we have. He raised up a man who had been dead four days, summoning him by His word alone. The dead man had begun to decay, and his body was corrupted by the worms and had the stench of a dog. However, seeing him lying in the tomb He commanded him to run. The dead man did not delay, but as a bridegroom out of his chamber, he ran from his tomb, smelling like perfume. He also cured strangers who were clearly demoniacs. These strangers dwelt in the deserts, and devoured their own cattle and all manner of creeping things. He turned them into inhibitors of cities, and by a word rendered them rational. He made them wise and powerful. He cast the unclean spirits into the depth of the sea.

There was another who had a withered hand. Not only did the man have a withered hand but half of his body was

133

like a stone. The body of the man was not the shape of a man at all. Jesus healed him with a word and rendered him whole. Jesus healed a woman who had an issue of blood for a long time and whose veins and arteries were exhausted. She did not bare the image of a human body and appeared as if she were dead. She was speechless, so that all the physicians of the district were unable to cure her. The physicians had given her no hope of life. When Jesus passed by she mysteriously received strength as he passed by the woman and His shadow fell upon her. She touched Him from behind on the hem of His garment as he passed by and immediately regained the strength in her exhausted limbs, as if she had never suffered from anything. She began to run alone towards Capernaum, her own city, and reached it in a six days.

This Jesus did other miracles greater than these. I have observed greater works of wonder done by Jesus than by the gods whom we worship. But Herod Antipas, Archelaus, Philip, Annas and Caiaphas, delivered him to me, telling me with a loud commotion, that I must bring Him to trial. Therefore, I commanded Him to be crucified. I first scourged Him, though I found no evil in Him.

When He was crucified, there was darkness over the entire world, and the sun was obscured for half a day, and the stars appeared, but no luster was seen in them. The world of the departed was swallowed up, so that the very sanctuary of the temple, as they call it, could no longer be seen. There appeared a chasm in the earth. There was rolling of successive thunders. Amid this terror the dead appeared rising again, as the Jews themselves bore witness. It was said that Abraham, Isaac, Jacob, the twelve patriarchs, Moses and Job, who had been dead for thousands of years, were seen among them. There were many that I myself saw appearing

134

in their body. They were lamenting over the Jews, because of the transgression which was committed by them.

The terror of the earthquake continued from the sixth hour until the ninth hour. When it was evening on the first day of the week, there came a sound from heaven, and the heaven became seven times more luminous than on all other days. At the third hour of the night the sun appeared more luminous than it had ever shown, lighting up the whole hemisphere. As lightning flashes suddenly came forth in a storm, so there were seen men who were lofty in stature and glory. These were a countless host crying out. Their voices were heard like loud thunder, "Jesus, who was crucified, is risen again. Come up from Hades all you who were enslaved in the ground."

The chasm in the earth had no bottom. It appeared as if the very foundations of the earth were exposed. Those that shouted in heaven waited in the body among the dead that were raised. He that raised up all the dead said, "Say to my disciples, 'He goeth before you into Galilee. There shall you see Him.'"

All that night the light continued to shine. Many of the Jews died in the chasm of the earth, being swallowed up, so that on the morrow most of those who had persecuted Jesus were nowhere to be found. Others saw the apparition of men rising from the dead whom none of us had ever seen. Only one synagogue of the Jews was left standing in Jerusalem itself, for they all disappeared in that ruin.

Therefore, feeling terror and trembling dreadfully, I have written what I saw at that time and sent it to your Excellency. I have inserted what was done against Jesus by the Jews and sent it to Caesar.

THE REPORT OF PONTIUS PILATE,

Governor of Judea, which was sent to Tiberius Caesar in Rome.

To the most potent, dreadful and divine Tiberius, from Pontius Pilate, Administer of the Eastern Province.

I have undertaken to communicate to you the present state of affairs, though I am possessed with much fear and trembling. I administered this province from Jerusalem where the temple of the Jews is located in your Eastern Province. The Jews delivered up to me a certain man called Jesus. They had many accusations against Him. They themselves could not convict Him in anything. However, they spoke of one Jewish heresy against Him. They told me He had said that the Sabbath was not a day of rest.

That man Jesus had performed many cures and other good works. He had caused the blind to see. He cleansed lepers. He raised the dead. He healed paralytics who could not move with the word of His mouth. He had replaced all their bones in their rightful places. He gave them strength to walk and run by His word alone. He did another more mighty work, which would have been strange even among our gods. He raised Lazarus from the dead, who had been dead four days, by commanding with His word alone that the dead man should be raised. His body was already corrupted by worms, which bred in his wounds. He commanded the fetid body, which lay in the grave, to run as bridegroom from his chamber. Lazarus ran forth from his grave, full of sweet perfume.

He healed some that were grievously afflicted by demons, and lived in desert places. They devoured the flesh

136

of their own limbs, and lived among creeping things and wild beasts. He caused them to dwell in cities in their own houses. By a word He made them reasonable, and caused them to become wise and honorable. When He healed those that were vexed by unclean spirits and demons, He sent those evil spirits into a herd of swine and then into the seas and were drowned. Another, who had a withered hand, and half of his body unsound, was made whole by a word alone.

There was a woman who had an issue of blood for a long time, so that all the joints of her bones were seen and shone through like glass. All the physicians had dismissed her without hope, but He healed her. As Jesus was passing by she touched, from behind, the hem of His garments, and in that very hour the strength of her body was restored. She was made whole, as if she had never had an affliction, and she began to run fast towards her own city of Paneas. All these things happened, but the Jews reported that Jesus did these things on the Sabbath. I saw that greater marvels had been wrought by Him than by the gods whom we worship. Herod, Archelaus, Philip, Annas and Caiaphas, delivered Him up to me to be tried. I commanded that He should be crucified because of the tumult among the Jews.

When He was crucified, darkness came over all the world. The sun was altogether hidden, and the sky appeared dark while it was yet day so that the stars were seen, though they still had their luster obscured. I suppose your Excellency is not unaware that in all the world they lighted their lamps from the sixth hour until evening. The moon, which was like blood, did not shine all night long, although it was full. The stars and Orion made lamentation over the Jews, because of the transgression committed by them. On the first day of the week, about the third hour of the night, the sun appeared, as *it had never shone before. The whole heaven became bright. As lightning comes in a storm, so certain men of lofty stature, in beautiful array, and of indescribable glory, appeared in the air, and a countless host of angels cried out and said, Glory to God in the highest, and on earth peace, good will among men.*

There came up from Hades all those who were in bondage in the depths of the earth. At the sound of their voices all the mountains and hills were moved, and the rocks were rent, and great chasms were made in the earth, so that the very depths of the abyss were visible.

Amid the terror, dead men were seen rising again, so that the Jews who saw it said, "We beheld Abraham, and Isaac, and Jacob and the twelve patriarchs, who died some two thousand five hundred years before, and we beheld Noah clearly in the body. All the multitude walked about and sang hymns to God with a loud voice, saying, "The Lord our God, who hath risen from the dead, hath made alive all the dead, and Hades He hath spoiled."

Therefore, my Lord King, all that night the light continued. However, many of the Jews died, and were swallowed up in the chasms that night, so that not even their bodies were found. Now I mean, that those who suffered were the Jews who spoke against Jesus.

Through that terror I was amazed and seized with great trembling. I ordered what had been done by them to be written, and I have sent it to your Mightiness.

PARADOSIS

When the report of Pilate reached Rome and was read to Caesar in the company of many, everyone was amazed that it was because of the lawless conduct of Pilate that the darkness and earthquakes came upon the whole world. Caesar was filled with anger and sent soldiers with orders to bring Pilate in chains. When he had been brought to Rome, and Caesar heard that Pilate was there, he sat down in the temple of the gods, with the whole senate, and members of his army, and all the great ones of his empire. He commanded Pilate to come forward and said to him, "How could you do such a thing, you most impious one, when you had seen such great signs concerning that man? By your wicked daring you have destroyed the whole world."

Pilate answered, "Almighty Caesar, I am innocent of these things. It is the multitude of the Jews who are the guilty instigators." Caesar asked, "Who are they?" Pilate said, "Herod, Archelaus, Philip, Annas, Caiaphas and all the multitude of the Jews." Caesar said, "Why did you follow their advice?" Pilate answered, "This nation is rebellious and does not submit to your power." Caesar said, "As soon as they handed Him over to you, you should have kept Him secure and sent Him to me and not have followed them by crucifying such a righteous man who did such wonderful signs as you have mentioned in your report. For it is clear from these signs that Jesus was the Christ, the King of the Jews."

When Caesar said this, and named the name of Christ, all the gods fell down where Caesar sat with the senate and became as dust. All the people who stood by Caesar trembled at the fall of their gods by reason of the naming of the name of Christ. Gripped by fear, they all went away, each to his own house, marveling at what had taken place. Caesar commanded that Pilate should be kept in custody in order that he might learn the truth about Jesus. On the next day, Caesar sat in the capitol with all the senate so he could continue to question Pilate.

Caesar said, "Speak the truth, you most impious man, for through your godless behavior against Jesus, the working of your crime was made manifest even here in the overthrow of our gods. Tell me now! Who crucified the one whose name destroyed all the gods?" Pilate answered, "Truly the charges made against Him are true. For I myself was convinced by His deeds that He is greater than all the gods whom we worship." Caesar said, "Why then did you treat Him with such wickedness when you already knew Him. In doing this you must have wished to harm my kingdom." Pilate answered, "I did it because of the insubordination of the lawless and godless Jews."

Then Caesar, filled with anger, took counsel with all the senate and his army and ordered the following decree to be recorded against the Jews.

To Licianus, Chief Governor of the East: Greetings

At the present time, the Jews who live in Jerusalem and the neighboring towns have committed a lawless crime in forcing Pilate to crucify Jesus who was acknowledged as God. Because of their crime, the world was darkened and dragged down to ruin. Therefore, by this decree proceed there with all speed with a strong body of troops and take them prisoner. Obey, and advance against them dispersing them among all the nations. Enslave them and expel them from Judea, making the nation so insignificant that it is no longer to be seen anywhere, since they are men full of evil.

When this decree arrived in the east, Licianus carried out his terrible instructions and destroyed the whole Jewish nation. *Those who were left in Judea, he scattered as slaves among the nations so that Caesar was pleased when he learned of the actions of Licianus against the Jews in the East. Again Caesar questioned Pilate, and commanded and officer called Albius to behead him saying, "As this man raised his hand against the Righteous Man called Christ so do I raise my hand against him."*

When Pilate came to the place of execution, he prayed silently, "Lord, do not destroy me with the wicked Hebrews. For it was through the lawless nations of the Jews that I raised my hand against you because they plotted a revolt against me. You know that I acted in ignorance. Therefore, do not condemn me because of this sin. Pardon me, Lord, and your servant. Procula, whom God made to prophesy that He must be nailed to the cross and who stands by me at the hour of my death. Do not condemn her also because of my sins. Pardon us, and number us among your righteous ones.

When Pilate had finished his prayer, there sounded a voice from heaven, "All generations and families of the gentiles shall call you blessed. Because in your Governorship all was fulfilled which the prophets foretold about me. You yourself shall appear as my witness at my Second Coming when I shall judge the twelve tribes of Israel and those who have not confessed my name."

At that moment the Prefect cut off the head of Pilate. Behold, an angel of the Lord received it. When Procula, his wife, saw the angel coming, and receiving his head, she was filled with joy and immediately gave up the ghost and was buried with her husband.

THE WITNESS OF ANANIAS AND THE WRITINGS OF NICODEMUS

I, Ananias, an officer of the Roman guard, being learned in the law, came to know our Lord Jesus Christ from the sacred scriptures, which I approached with faith and was accounted worthy of holy baptism. I searched for the reports made at that period of time concerning our Lord Jesus Christ and found these writings about the Jews while they were under the Governorship of Pontius Pilate. I found these acts in the Hebrew language, and according to God's good pleasure, I translated them into Greek for the information of all those who call upon the name of our Lord Jesus Christ in the eighteenth year of the reign of our emperor Flavius Thaeodosius, and in the fifth year of the nobility of Flavius Valentinianus in the ninth indiction. Therefore, all you who read this, and copy it out, remember me and pray for me that God may be gracious to me and
forgive my sins, which I have sinned against him. Peace be to those who read and hear it, and to their servants, amen.

In the nineteenth year of the reign of the Roman Emperor Tiberius, when Herod was king of Galilee, when Joseph Caiaphas was Chief Priest of the Jews, Nicodemus, after the passion of the Lord upon the cross, recorded and delivered these things concerning the conduct of the Chief Priest and the rest of the Jews. The same Nicodemus drew up his records in the Hebrew language.

THE WRITINGS OF NICODEMUS

Pilate, the Governor, said unto his messenger, "Go forth and bring Jesus to the Praetorium." The messenger went forth and said, "Lord, come in, for the Governor calls you." As Jesus was going in the great room, He passed by the ensigns who carried the standards, the tops of which bowed down and worshiped Jesus. Whereupon the Sadducees exclaimed vehemently against the ensigns. However, Pilate said to the Sadducees, "I know it is not pleasing to you that the tops of the standards did of themselves bow and worship Jesus. However, why do you protest against the ensigns, as if they had bowed their standards in worship?"

The Sadducees replied to Pilate, "We saw the ensigns themselves bowing the standards of themselves to worship Jesus." The Governor called the ensigns and said unto them, "Why did you do this?" The ensigns said to Pilate, "We are all pagans and worship our own gods in our temples. Why should we think anything about worshiping this Jesus? We only held the standards in our hands and they bowed by themselves and worshipped Him. The standards themselves aid Pilate before the Rulers of the synagogue." Then Pilate said to the Sadducees, "Go yourselves and choose some strong men and let them hold the standards. Then we all shall see whether the standards will bend of themselves."

So the elders of the Sadducees sought out twelve of their strongest and able men and made them hold the standards as they all stood in the presence of the Governor. Then Pilate said to his messenger, "Take Jesus out and bring Him in again." Jesus and the messenger went out of the hall. Pilate called the ensigns, who no longer held the standards, and swore to them, "If they the standards do not bow as before when Jesus comes in, I will cut off your heads." Then the Governor commanded Jesus to come in again. The messenger did as he had done before, and strongly petitioned Jesus that he would walk upon his own cloak, which he had spread upon the floor. Jesus walked upon the messenger's cloak and returned back into the Preatorium. When Jesus entered in, the standards bowed as before, and worshipped Him.

NICODEMUS CONTINUED

When the Sadducees had heard that Joseph of Arimathea had asked for the body of Jesus from Pilate, they sought after him and the twelve apostles. Nicodemus, and many others, who had stood before Pilate, hid themselves in the synagogue. Only Nicodemus stood before them to be seen. Nicodemus was a Ruler among the Jews. Nicodemus said to the Sadducees who had come, "How did you enter the synagogue?" The Sadducees answered him, "How did you enter the synagogue? You are an accomplice of Joseph who asked for the body of Jesus and his portion of blame shall be with you in the world to come." Nicodemus said, "Amen Amen."

At that moment, Joseph of Arimathea came forward from his place of concealment and said to the Sadducees, who were looking for him, "Why are you angry with me because I asked for the body of Jesus? I have placed it in my own tomb, having wrapped it in clean linen and I rolled a stone before the door of the cave. You have not done well with that righteous one, having crucified Him and pierced with a spear."

Then the Sadducees seized Joseph and imprisoned him until the first day of the week. The Sadducees said to Joseph on his way to the prison, "The hour forbids us to do anything against you because the Sabbath draws near. Know, however, that when we return, you will not even be counted worthy of burial. We shall give your flesh to birds of the heavens." Joseph answered the Sadducees saying, "Your words are like the boast of Goliath who insulted the living God and the holy David. For God said, 'Vengeance is mine.' (Romans 12:19 cf. Deut. 32:35) You saw that Pilate, who is uncircumcised in the flesh but circumcised in heart, took water and washed his hands before Jesus and the multitudes and said, 'I am innocent of the blood of this righteous man. If He must be crucified you do it.' It was then that you, the Sadducees, answered Pilate, 'His blood be on us and our children.' (Matt 27:25) 'Now I fear lest the wrath of God come upon you and your children according to your own words.'"

When the Sadducees heard these words they became bitter in their hearts and laid hold of Joseph and shut him in a building without a window and only one door. Guards were placed at the door and the prison door was sealed.

On the Sabbath the Rulers of the synagogue and the priests and the Levites ordered that all should present themselves in the synagogue on the first day of the week. The whole multitude rose up early on the first day and took counsel in the synagogue concerning how Joseph should be killed. When the council was in session, they commanded Joseph to be brought before them with great dishonor. When they opened the door that had been sealed, Joseph was gone. All these great people were astonished and were filled with consternation because they found their seals to the door undamaged. Caiaphas alone had the keys to the prison door. None of them any longer dared to lay hands on those who had spoken before Pilate on behalf of Jesus.

While they still sat in the synagogue and marveled because of Joseph, there arrived some of the guards, which had guarded the tomb of Jesus. They told the Rulers of the synagogue and the priests and the Levites what had happened at the tomb of Jesus. They began by saying, "There was a great earthquake. We saw an angel descend from heaven and he rolled away the stone from the mouth of the cave and sat upon it. He shown like the snow and like the lightening from heaven. We were in great fear and lay on the ground like dead men. (Matt 28: 2-4) Then we heard the voice of the angel speaking to the women who waited at the tomb to not be afraid. We heard the angel say, 'I know that you seek Jesus who was crucified. He is not here. He has risen as He said. Come and see the place where the Lord lay. Go quickly and tell His disciples He has risen from the dead and is in Galilee.'" (Matt 28: 5-7)

The Chief Priests and the other Sadducees asked the Roman soldiers, "To what women did He speak?" The members of the guard answered, "We do not know who they were." The Sadducees then inquired, "At what hour of the day did these things happen?" They answered, "At midnight." The Sadducees continued, "Why did you not seize the women?" The guard said, "We were like dead men from fear and gave up hope of ever seeing the light of day. How could we then have seized them?"

The Sadducees turned from the guards and said, "As the Lord lives, we do not believe you." The guards in similar fashion turned their heads and replied to the

Sadducees, "You have seen many signs performed by Jesus and yet you did not believe. Why should we expect that you should believe us now? You were right when you swore 'as the Lord lives,' for He does live. We have heard that you shut up Joseph of Arimathea who asked for the body of Jesus and sealed the door behind him. When you opened it again you did not find him. Therefore, we will make you a bargain. Give us Joseph of Arimathea and we will give you Jesus." The Sadducees said, "Joseph has gone to his own city." The Roman guards likewise retorted to the Sadducees, "An angel has told us that Jesus has risen from his tomb and is in Galilee."

When the Sadducees had heard these words, they became afraid and said, "Take heed lest your report be heard and all that hear it be inclined to believe in Jesus and His resurrection." The Sadducees took counsel and offered the guards a great sum of money and said to them, "Say that when you were sleeping, His disciples came by night and stole His body from the tomb. If this is heard by the Governor, we will persuade him to keep you out of trouble." (Matt 28: 12-14)

Now Phinees a priest, and Adas a teacher, and Angaeus a Levite, came from Galilee to Jerusalem and told the Rulers of the synagogue and the priests and the Levites, "We saw Jesus and His disciples sitting upon the mountain called Mamilch. He said to His disciples, 'Go to all the world and preach the gospel to all creation. He who believes and is baptized will be saved. He who does not believe will be condemned. These signs will accompany those who believe in my name. They will cast out demons. They will speak in new tongues. They will pick up deadly serpents and not die. If they drink any deadly thing it will not hurt them. They will lay their hands on the sick and they will recover.' (Mark 16: 15-18) While Jesus was still speaking to His disciples, we saw Him taken up into heaven.'"

Then the elders and priests and the Levites said, "Give glory to the God of Israel. Confess before Him if you indeed heard and saw what you have described." Then these men from Galilee said, "As the Lord God of our fathers, Abraham, Isaac, and Jacob live, we heard these things and saw Him taken up to heaven."

The elders and priests and Levites said to them, "Did you come to tell us this, or did you come offer prayer to God." They answered, "To offer prayer to God." The elders and the Chief Priests and the Levites said to them, "If you come to offer prayer to God, to what purpose is the idle tale which you have babbled before all the people." The men from Galilee said to the Rulers of the synagogue, "The words which we spoke concerning what we heard and saw are sin before you. Do with us as its seems good in your eyes." The Sadducees then bade them to not tell these things to anyone. Then they gave the soldiers to eat and drink and sent them out of the city, having given them money and three of their own men to accompany them till they had left the city. The Sadducees ordered them to depart as far a Galilee. So the guards went away in peace.

When the guards had departed to Galilee, the Rulers and some of the elders assembled in the synagogue and shut the gates behind them and raised a great lamentation saying, "Why has this sign happened in Israel?" Annas and Caiaphas then said loudly to the Rulers and elders lamenting in the synagogue, "Why are you troubled? Why do you weep? Do you not know that Jesus' disciples gave money to the guards of the tomb and then took away His body and told them to say that an angel descended from heaven and rolled away the stone from the entrance." The Rulers and the elders replied, "Then let us say, to appease the argument, that His disciples stole His body, but how did His soul enter again into that body so that Jesus now waits in Galilee?" The Sadducees were unable to give an answer and with some difficulty said to the Rulers and the elders, "In any case, it is not lawful for us to believe the uncircumcised."

It was then that Nicodemus returned to the conversation and stood up before the Sadducees and said, "What these men, who you have sent away, have said is right. You know these men who came from Galilee and that they fear God and are men of substance, righteousness and peace. They have declared on oath, 'We saw Jesus on the mountain Mamilch with His disciples.' Jesus Himself taught them what you have heard from them. They saw Him taken into heaven and no one asked them at the time what manner He was taken up."

Then the Sadducees sent to every mountain of Israel and searched for Jesus and did not find Him. However, they found Joseph in Arimathea at his home and no one dared to seize him. The messengers of the Sadducees told the elders the priests and the Levites, "We went about to every mountain of Israel and did not find Jesus, but Joseph we found in Arimathea."

When the Rulers of the synagogue and the elders heard about Joseph, they rejoiced and gave glory to the God of Israel and they took counsel of how they should meet with Joseph. They took a roll of papyrus and wrote to Joseph these words:

"Peace be with you. We know that we have sinned against God and against you. We have prayed to the God of Israel that you should condescend to come to us because we are all troubled. For when we opened the door we did not find you. We know that we devised an evil plan against you. But the Lord helped you. The Lord Himself has brought to nothing our plan against you, honored father Joseph."

Then the Sadducees chose from all Israel, seven men who were well known friends of Joseph. The Rulers of the synagogue said to the friends of Joseph, "If he receives our letter and reads it, know that he will come with you to us; but if he does not read it, know that he is angry with us and salute him in peace and return to us." They blessed the men and dismissed them.

When the seven friends of Joseph found him in Arimathea, they greeted him with reverence and said to him, "Peace be with you." He replied, "Peace be with you and all Israel." They gave to him the roll of the letter. Joseph took it and read it and kissed the letter and blessed God and said, "Blessed be God that has delivered the Israelites from the shedding of innocent blood. Blessed be the Lord who sent His angel and sheltered me under His wings."

Then Joseph set a table before his seven friends and they ate and drank and lay down to sleep. They rose up early in the morning and prayed. Joseph saddled his she-ass and went with his friends to Jerusalem.

When they arrived at the holy city of Jerusalem, all the people met Joseph and cried, "Peace be at your coming." He said to all the people, "Peace be with you." All of the people who met him kissed him and prayed with Joseph and were beside themselves with joy at seeing him. Nicodemus received him into his house and made a great feast. He called the Rulers and elders to his house and they made merry, eating and drinking with Joseph. After singing a hymn, each one went to his house, but Joseph remained in the house of Nicodemus.

On the next day, which was the day of preparation for the Sabbath, the Rulers of the synagogue, Sadducees and the Levites rose up early and came to the house of Nicodemus. Nicodemus met them and said, "Peace be with you." They answered, "Peace be with you and with Joseph and with all your house" and Nicodemus brought them into his house.

The whole council sat down and Joseph sat between Annas and Caiaphas. No one dared to speak a word to Joseph. Joseph finally asked of them, "Why have you called me?" They beckoned to Nicodemus, "Speak to Joseph for us." Nicodemus opened his mouth and said to Joseph, "Father, you know that the honorable teachers and Chief Priests and Levites wish information from you." Joseph answered, "Then ask me."

Annas and Caiaphas took the books of the law in their hands and inquired of Joseph saying, "It is written, give glory to the God of Israel and make concession to Him. For Achan also, when asked by the prophet Joshua, did not commit perjury, but told him everything and concealed nothing from him." (Joshua 7) "So also do not conceal from us a single word." Joseph answered, "I will not conceal anything from you." Then the Sadducees said to Joseph, "We were very angry because you asked for the body of

Jesus and wrapped it in a clean linen cloth and placed it in your tomb. For this reason we secured you in a house with no windows and locked and sealed the doors behind you. We placed guards at the door where you were shut up. On the first day of the week, we opened it and did not find you. Seeing that you were gone, we were much troubled. All the people of God have since been amazed until yesterday when you arrived here in Jerusalem. Now tell us what happened to you."

Joseph said, "On the day of preparation, about the tenth hour, you shut me in and I remained the whole of next day which was the Sabbath. At midnight, as I stood and prayed, the house where you shut me in was raised up by the four corners and I saw, as it were, a lightening flash in my eyes. Full of fear, I fell to the ground. Someone took me by the hand and raised me up from the place where I had fallen. Something moist like water flowed from my head to my feet. The smell of fragrant oil reached my nostrils. He wiped my face and kissed me. He said to me, 'Do not fear, Joseph. Open your eyes to see who it is who speaks with you.' I looked up and saw Jesus. Trembling, I thought it was a devil, and I began to say the Ten Commandments. He said them with me. Now, as you all well know, a devil immediately flees from anyone who is saying the Ten Commandments. When I saw that He said them with me, I said to Him 'Rabbi Elijah!' He said, 'I am not Elijah.' I said to Him, 'Who are you, Lord?' He replied, 'I am Jesus, whose body you asked for from Pilate, whom you clothed in clean linen, on whose face you placed the cloth and whom you placed in your new cave and you rolled a great stone to the door of the cave.'"

"I asked Him who spoke to me, 'Show me the place

where I laid you.' He took me with Him to the place where I had laid Jesus. The linen cloth, in which I had wrapped the body of Jesus, lay there on the floor of the tomb along with the cloth that was on His face. Then I recognized that it was Jesus. He took me by the hand and placed me in the middle of my house with the doors shut and led me to my bed and said to me, 'Peace be with you.' He kissed me and said to me, 'Do not go out of your house for forty days for see I go to my brethren in Galilee.'"

When the Rulers of the synagogue and the priests and the Levites heard these words from Joseph, they became as dead men and fell to the ground and fasted till the ninth hour. Nicodemus and Joseph confronted Annas and Caiaphas and the priests and the Levites saying, "Get up and stand on your feet and taste bread and strengthen your souls, for tomorrow is the Sabbath of the Lord." They rose up and prayed to God and ate and drank and each of them went each to his own house.

On the Sabbath all returned again and began to question one another saying, "What is this wrath which has come upon us? We knew Jesus' father and His mother." Levi, the teacher, said, "I knew that His parents feared God and did not withhold their prayers and paid tithes three times a year. When Jesus was born, His parents brought him to this very place and gave God sacrifices and burnt offerings. When Jesus' parents brought Him to this synagogue, the great teacher Symeon took Him in his arms and said, 'Lord, now let your servant depart in peace according to your word. For my eyes have seen your salvation which you have prepared in the presence of all people, a light for revelation to the gentiles and for glory to your people of Israel.'"

Symeon blessed them and said to Mary His mother, "I give you good tidings concerning this child." Mary said, "It is well my lord." Symeon then said to her, "Behold this child is set for the fall and rising of many in Israel. As a sign, a sword will pierce through your own soul that thoughts, out of many hearts, may be revealed to you." (Luke 2: 28-35)

The Sadducees asked Levi the teacher, "How do you know these things?" Levi answered them; "Do you not know that I learned the law from Jesus." The council said to Him, "We wish to see your father." They sent for his father. When they questioned his father, he said to them, "Why did you not believe my son?"

THE TESTIMONIES OF TWO RESURRECTED BEINGS

There were many other witnesses that were called by the Rulers of the Synagogue and who testified that Jesus had risen from the dead in the larger writings of Nicodemus. However, there are two witnesses that are of particular importance.

The Sadducees sent to Galilee and called for their servants to bring with them the two resurrected men who they had known while they were alive and who had been seen still walking the streets of Galilee. These two resurrected men were the sons of Symeon the priest, who had taken the place of Zacharias who was murdered. The messengers of the Sadducees walking in Arimathea found the sons of Symeon, Charinus and Lenthius. Charinus and Lenthius returned with the messengers to Jerusalem and sat before Caiaphas and Annas and the Rulers of the

154

Synagogue and testified in two separate rooms that they had been risen from the dead and had been present when Jesus descended into the world of the spirits and saw Him raise the spirits from that world. Each of them signed their testimonies separately in two books that were sealed and Joseph of Arimathea took one of those books and Caiaphas and Annas the other. Joseph took his book and showed it to Pilate and later took his book with him in exile to England. Their testimonies were as follows:

"I, Charinus and Lenthius, are not allowed to declare the other mysteries of God, as the Arch Angel Michael had ordered. Saying, "You shall go with my brethren to Jerusalem and shall continue in prayers, declaring and glorifying the resurrection of Jesus Christ, seeing He has raised you from the dead at the same time with Himself and you shall not talk with any man but sit as dumb persons till the time come when the Lord will allow you to relate mysteries of His divinity."

"The Arch Angel Michael further commanded us to go beyond Jordan to an excellent and fat country where there are many who rose from the dead with us. For we have only three days allowed us from the dead to celebrate the Passover of our Lord with our families and to bear our testimony of Christ the Lord. And we have been baptized in the holy river of Jordan. This is as much as God allowed us to relate to you. Therefore, give praise and honor to Him and repent and He will have mercy upon you. Peace be to you from the Lord God Jesus, the Savior of us all, Amen Amen."

After they had made an end of writing and had written on two distinct pieces of paper, Charinus gave what he wrote into the hands of Annas and Caiaphas and Gamalial. Lenthius likewise gave what he wrote into the hands of Nicodemus and Joseph and immediately were changed into exceedingly white forms and were seen no more, but what they had written was found perfectly to agree, one paper not containing one letter more or less than the other.

THE HEALING OF TIBERIUS CAESAR

Now whereas Tiberius Caesar, Emperor of the Romans, was suffering from a grievous sickness and hearing that there was at Jerusalem a certain physician, Jesus by name, who healed all diseases by His word alone, not knowing that the Jews and Pilate had put Him to death. He therefore called one of his attendants, Volusianus by name, saying, "Go as quickly as you can across the sea and tell Pilate my servant and friend to send me this physician to restore me to my original health."

Volusianus, having heard the order of the Emperor, immediately departed and came to Pilate as he was commanded. He told Pilate what had been committed to him by Tiberius Caesar saying, "Tiberius Caesar, Emperor of the Romans, your Lord having heard that in this city there is a physician who heals diseases by His word alone, earnestly entreats you to send Jesus to him to heal his diseases." Pilate was greatly terrified when he heard this, knowing that he had caused Jesus to be slain. Pilate answered the messenger saying, "This man was a malefactor and a man who drew after Himself all the people. So after counsel taken of the wise men of the city, I caused Him to be crucified."

As the messenger returned to his lodging, he met a certain women named Veronica, who had been acquainted with Jesus and he said, "O woman, there was a certain physician in this city who healed the sick by His word alone. Why have the Jews slain Him?" She began to weep saying, "He was not my Lord, He was my God, and Pilate delivered Him up and commanded Him to be crucified." Then Volusianus grieving greatly said, "I am exceedingly sorry that I can not fulfill the mission of Tiberius Caesar who sent me."

Veronica said to him, "When my Lord went about preaching, I was very unwillingly deprived of His presence. I desired to have His picture painted for me, so that while I was deprived of His presence at least the figure of His likeness might give me consultation. When I was taking the canvas to the painter to be painted, my Lord met me in the way and asked where I was going. When I had made known to Him the cause of my Journey, He asked me for the canvas and gave it back to me printed with the likeness of His venerable face. Therefore, if Caesar will devoutly look upon this likeness, he will straightway enjoy the benefit of health." "Is a likeness of this kind to be procured with gold or silver?" he asked. "No," said she, but with a sentiment of devotion. "Therefore, I will go with you and carry the likeness to Caesar to look upon and then I will return."

So Volusianus came with Veronica to Rome and said to Tiberius the Emperor, "Jesus, whom you have long desired from Pilate, has been surrendered by the Jews to an unjust death and fashioned to the wood of the cross. Therefore, a certain matron has come with me and brought the likeness of the same Jesus, and if you will devotedly gaze upon it, you will presently obtain the benefits of health." So Caesar caused a way to be spread with cloths of silk and ordered the portrait to be presented to him. As soon as he had looked upon it, he regained his original health.

THIS OLD MAN'S THOUGHT

There is a still small voice inside us all that leads men to truth. The only barrier to hearing it is the doubt one feels within oneself--for oneself. All the rest that follows is mere discovery. Belief does not make things exist, but truth is worth nothing without it.

BIBLIOGRAPHY

- Angus, S., The Mystery Religions and Christianity, New York, 1925
- Bammel, E., Christian Origins in Tradition, New Testament Studies, 1967
- Barnstone, W., The Other Bible, New York, 1984
- Bayer, W., Orthodoxy and Heresy in Earliest Christianity, Philadelphia, 1971
- Black, M., The Scrolls and Christian Origins, New York, 1961
- Blinzler, J., The Trial of Jesus: Jewish and Roman Proceedings Against Jesus Christ, Translation I. and F. McHugh, 2nd rev. ed., Westminster, Md, 1959
- Brown, R. E., The Death of the Messiah: From Gethsemane to the Grave, New York, 1994
- Brown, R. E., The Gospel According to John, New York, 1966
- Carsten, Peter, Theide, Matthew, D-Ancona, The Eye Witnesses to Jesus, Doubleday, 1996
- Catchpole, David R., The trial of Jesus: A Study in the Gospels and Jewish Historiography from 1770 to the Present Day, Leiden: Brill 1971
- Cross, F. L., ed The Jung Codex, a Newly Recovered Gnostic Papyrus
- Dunstan, Victor, Did the Virgin Mary Live and Die in England: South Wales England 1985
- Three Studies, London, 1955

- Frend, W.H.C., Martyrdom and Persecution in the Early Church
- Goodspeed, E.J., The Story of the Apocrypha, Chicago, 1939
- Grayzel, S., A History of the Jews, Philadelphia, 1947
- Harnack, A., The Mission and Expansion of Christianity in the First Three Centuries, 2 vols, New York, 1908
- Hennecke, E. Schneemelcher, W. New Testament Apocrypha (Translation from Neutestamentliche Apocryphen), Philadelphia, 1963
- Himmelfard, M., Tours of Hell: An Apocalyptic Form in Jewish and Christian Literature, Philadelphia 1983
- Hirsch, E. G., The Crucifixion from the Jewish Point of View, Chicago, 1921
- Husband, R. W., The Prosecution of Jesus: It's Date, History and Legality, Princeton 1916
- Josephus, The Jewish War Loeb edition, vol 2, translation H. St. J. Thackery, London, 1926
- Jowett, George F., The Drama of the Lost Disciples, London, 1993
- Klausner, J., Jesus von Nazareth, Seine Zeit, Seine Leben und Seine Lehre, 2nd ed., Berlin, 1934
- Lindars, B., New Testament Apologetic: The Doctrinal Significance of the Old Testament Quotations, London, 1973

- McGinny, B. C., The Governorship of Pontius Pilate: Messiahs and Sources, Proceedings of the Irish Biblical Ass. (1986)
- MacMullen, R., Brigandage appendix B in Enemies of the Roman Order: Treason, Unrest, and Alienation in the Empire, Cambridge, Mass. 1967
- Metzger, B.M., An Introduction to the Apocrypha, New York, 1957
- Miller, Robert J., ed The Complete Gospels: Annotated Scholars Version San francisco, 1992
- Montefiori, C., The Synoptic Gospels I, 2nd rev. ed., London, 1927
- Montefiori, C., Lectures on the Origin and Growth of Religion and Illustrated by the Religion of the Ancient Hebrews, London, 1892
- Moore, G. F., Judaism in the First Centuries of the Christian Era, 2 vols, New York, 1971
- Nineham, D., The Gospel of St. Mark, Baltimore, 1967
- Pagels, E., The Johannine Gospel in Gnostic Exegesis, Nashville, 1973
- Pagels, E., The Origin of Satan, New York, 1995
- Porter, F. C., The Messages of the Apocalyptical Writers, London 1905
- Radin, M., The Trial of Jesus of Nazareth, Chicago, 1931
- Reuther, R. Faith and Fratricide: The Theological. Roots of Anti Semitism, Minneapolis, 1974
- Robinson, J. M., ed. The Nag Hammadi Library in English, Leiden: Brill 1977
- Ryan, T.J., ed Critical History and Biblical Faith: New Testament Perspectives, Villanova, 1979
- Sanders, E.P., Jesus and Judaism, Philadelphia, 1985

- Schneenelcher, Wilhelm, ed. New Testament Apocrypha, translation R. McL. Wilson, Philadelphia: Westminster, 1963
- Scholer, David M., Nag Hammadi Bibliography 1948-1969, Leiden: Brill, 1971
- Scharer, E., History of the Jewish People in the Time of Jesus, 5 vols. Edinburgh, 1885-91; New York 1938
- Schweitzer, A., The Quest of the Historical Jesus: A Critical Study of it's Progress from Reimarus to Wrede, London, 1926
- Sherwin-White, A.N., Roman Society and Roman Law in the New testament, Oxford, 1983
- Sloyan, G.S., Jesus on Trial: The Narratives and Their Historical and Ecumenical Implications, Philadelphia, 1973
- Smallwood, M., The Jew Under Roman Rule from Pompeii to Diocletian, Leiden: Brill 1981
- Stauffer, E., "Aur Munzpragung des Pontius Pilate," La Nouvelle Clio 1-2 (1949-50)
- Stendahl, K., The School of St. Matthew, Uppsala, 1954
- The Lost Books of the Bible, World Bible Pub., 1926
- Van Unnik, W.C., Newly discovered Gnostic Writings, London, 1960
- Winter, P., On the Trial of Jesus, 2nd ed. Berlin, 1974
- Zandee, J. The terminology of Plotinus and Some Gnostic Writings, Mainly the Fourth Treatise of the Jung Codex, Istanbul, 1961